INSTANT CHICAGO
how to cope

by Jory Graham

RAND McNALLY & COMPANY
Chicago • New York • San Francisco

Quotation from "Action Line," p. 91, reprinted with permission from *Chicago Today;* from "Beeline," pp. 91–92, reprinted with permission from *Chicago Daily News;* IPO material, p. 131, from "Jory Graham's City," reprinted with permission from *Chicago Sun-Times*

Other Books by Jory Graham

Katie's Zoo

Children on a Farm

I'm Driving My Analyst Crazy

Chicago: An Extraordinary Guide

Library of Congress Catalog Card Number: 79-182931

Printed in the United States of America
by Rand McNally & Company

ISBN: 0-528-81809-0

First printing, 1973

CONTENTS

ACKNOWLEDGMENTS

These thoughtful human beings enriched this book. I thank them all.

Consultants

Warner G. Baird, Jr.
Wayne A. Benjamin
Ald. Leon M. Despres
Robert Eck
Sam S. Fawley
James A. FitzSimmons, D.D.S.
Jayne FitzSimmons
Max Forman, M.D.
Melvin V. Gerbie, M.D.
Cary Lynn Gray
Betty M. Hahneman, M.D.
Mac Hansborough
Barbara Harris
Cecil W. Hart, M.D.
Jay G. Housten
Elinor and Wellington Hummel
Julian H. Levi

Jack M. Levin
Lawrence F. Levy
Franklin Lounsbury, M.D.
Anne Macauley
Patricia McCreary, M.D.
Richard D. Nirenberg
Maxine Noonan
Harry M. Oliver
Marshall Patner
Herbert Reis
Ralph A. Reis, M.D.
Eric Schaps
Eric H. Steele
Mitchell S. Watkins
Jerome E. Wexler
Jack Witkowsky
Rita B. Yacker

Contributing Editors

Betty Brennan, Allen Van Cranebrock, Jr.

Contributor

Talmage Mullen Steele for the lucid section "Evaluating a Public School"

Super Researchers

Susan Sinykin Benjamin, Barbara Berger, Katharine M. Fansler,
Beata M. Hayton, Judith R. Housten, Patricia Kuehn

Secretaries

Lorraine Marie Minkus, Michal Ann Schafer

Index

William H. Frazer

Maps

Rand McNally

CHICAGO, CHICAGO

What's Chicago? It's a city, six counties, more than 250 suburbs, almost seven-million people—the most dynamic metropolitan center in America in the 1970s.

People move here because opportunity is here. So are the advantages of museums, universities, medical centers, the greatest symphony orchestra, opera, theatre, restaurants, shops. The city's alive and vital; the suburbs are exploding in growth.

To live in metropolitan Chicago is to accept challenge—and be willing to cope. Cope on a daily basis with rush hour traffic and pollution. Cope with the mayor, the machine, the police. Cope with discrimination in housing and jobs. Cope with a slew of unresponsive local bureaucracies.

People have human problems wherever they live, but in this enormous urban complex they can't be expected to know where to turn for help.

That's why I wrote this handbook.

If you're a newcomer, it can help you come to grips with the essentials —find a pleasant place to live, learn about schools, know where to turn in emergencies, find a physician who can become your doctor.

It tackles the problems residents contend with—pitfalls in leases and in new suburban home developments, local rackets, consumer fraud.

It tells you what you can legitimately expect from your alderman and how to cut through the snarls of city, county, and state red tape.

It looks at alternatives to public schools (most private school tuitions are staggering) and shows how concerned parents can make inroads against gross deficiencies in public schools their children attend.

It helps with practical matters—insurance, mortgage loans, baby-sitters, nursery schools, cleaning ladies, repairmen.

It goes into the problem of finding a decent nursing home for an aging parent and shows how to cope if you have to settle for what you can afford.

People get into trouble—drugs, VD, alcohol, an unwanted pregnancy, the law. This book helps with these. It also leads you to competent sources for help with physical handicaps and emotional problems.

And it suggests ways to not be lonely, new ways to make friends.

Chicago is rewarding when you know your way around, feel you belong.

With all best wishes,

JORY GRAHAM

CHICAGOESE

Standard English pronunciation of *Chicago* is *Shi-CAH-go*. Do not use Mayor Daley's pronunciation, as in "Dis great city of Tsch-caw-ga." The mayor is a man who grapples with his native tongue as if it were a confrontation.

Another classic example of Chicagoese is columnist Mike Royko's quote of City Hall patronage workers referring to their mayor as "da mare." Royko is not being smart-ass; he simply has an excellent ear.

To the astonishment of all British living here, *Devon*, the name of a street on the far North Side of the city, is pronounced *De-VON*.

Despite the city's strong German heritage, almost no Chicagoan correctly pronounces *Goethe*, the name of a short but important Near North Side street. Ask your cabby to take you to Guth, Go-eeth, Goaty, Go-eeth-ee, or Goth or ask for the Ambassador East Hotel and you'll make it.

The French heritage in Chicago is even more remote. Hence, *Des Plaines* —the name of a suburb, an avenue, a local river, and a street in the city proper—is always pronounced *Dezz PLAINS*. Don't try to show off your French; nobody will know what you're talking about. In print, the suburb, avenue, and river are written Des Plaines, the street Desplaines.

SEMANTICS I

North Side, South Side, West Side	Originally defined by the Chicago River and its branches. Now, rather amorphous areas identified only by their direction from the Loop.
Near North	To most people, the glittering status strip of the city from the Chicago River to North Avenue, between Lake Michigan and LaSalle Street. In fact, its boundaries extend west to the North Branch of the Chicago River through some of the worst poverty in the city.
Mid North	Imprecisely defined area that everyone assumes he knows precisely. Roughly, from North Avenue to Diversey, Lincoln Park west to DePaul University neighborhood.
Midtown	Synonym for Mid North, more or less.
Old Town	To tourists, the section of Wells Street between Goethe and Menomonee. Residents of the real Old Town, a small area of charming residential streets, wouldn't be found dead on it.
New Town	A strip of restaurants and young life-style shops on Broadway, from Diversey north to Belmont.

7

Uptown	What most people call a poor, shabby, multiracial subneighborhood around the intersection of Broadway and Lawrence.
Downtown	The Loop.
North Shore	Prestige suburbs immediately north of Chicago, along the lake from Evanston to Lake Bluff. By their own definition, adjacent Glenview, Northbrook, and Northfield are also part of the North Shore.
South Shore	Chicago between 67th and 79th Streets, from the lake west to approximately Stony Island Avenue. Also Chicagoese for a commuter railroad—Chicago, South Shore & South Bend.
The Loop	Chicago's central business district, bigger than the original area around which the downtown elevated tracks looped, hence the name. Present boundaries, Chicago River south to 12th Street, Michigan Avenue west to Desplaines Street.
The lake	Always means Lake Michigan.
The river	Always means the Chicago River.
Expressway	Same as a freeway in California and a throughway in New York.

SEMANTICS II

Aldermen	The 50 members of City Council; all but a handful are Democratic machine pols.
Boosterism	Excessive emphasis on superlatives: the biggest, the greatest, world's tallest, etc. "Magnificent Mile" for a less than one-mile stretch of North Michigan Avenue is a typical example.
Business	The *raison d'être* for Chicago. Hence, the official city attitude is "if it's good for business, leave it alone," which excuses everything from lax licensing practices to major land swindles.
Cabrini-Green, Robert Taylor Homes	Possibly the most ill-conceived public housing in the country. Always in the news because of excessive crime rate within. Cabrini-Green is located on the Near North Side, Robert Taylor Homes on the Near South Side.
Defensiveness	A pronounced native reaction to any criticism of the city.
Dog	What most landlords won't permit unless it's a yapping, midget variety, rarely obedience-trained or housebroken.
Cat	Scarcely more acceptable than a dog, though ownership of is easier to conceal.

Chicago Style	Sentimental, tough writing in the first person. Columnists Mike Royko (*Chicago Daily News*) and Tom Fitzpatrick (*Chicago Sun-Times*) are its current leading exponents. Studs Terkel on WFMT speaks Chicago Style.
Hizzoner	Mayor Daley.
Seiche	(rare) The equivalent of a tidal wave on the lake.

LOCAL ABBREVIATIONS

BGA	Better Government Association. Local watchdog organization generally recognized as the best of its kind in the country.
BPI	Businessmen for the Public Interest. Another reform-minded organization that's making an impact.
CAP	Citizens Action Program. Huge membership and effective.
Chicago A	Illinois Bell Telephone's alphabetical directory.
Yellow Pages B	Bell's directory for consumers.
Yellow Pages C	Bell's directory of industrial and commercial listings.
CPD	Chicago Police Department.
CHA	Chicago Housing Authority. An official city agency open to justified criticism for its failure to build desperately needed middle- and low-income housing and for its scandalous conflicts of interest.
CTA	Chicago Transit Authority—buses, subways, and elevated trains. Since some elevated trains go underground to become subways and some subways emerge on ascending tracks to become elevated trains, they're referred to collectively as the **Rapid Transit System.**
El or L	CTA elevated trains. In this book, spelled El.
4+1	Technically, four floors of wood-frame apartment construction (masked in stone or brick) on top of a small parking lot. The term is derogatory because one little sharpie found a way to sneak around Chicago's building code and erect airless, lightless, cheaply constructed housing for middle-income renters.
IC	Illinois Central Gulf Railroad, especially commuter trains to the South Side and beyond.
ICC	Illinois Commerce Commission. Regulatory agency governing rates of utilities, van lines, and the like. Fairly responsive to consumer complaints.
IPO & IVI	Two independent, reform-minded, generally liberal political organizations of growing strength. The

former is the Independent Precinct Organization, the latter the Independent Voters of Illinois.

MCA   Museum of Contemporary Art.

S/Ls   Savings & Loan Associations. Similar to banks—carry savings accounts but not checking accounts. Pay ¼% more interest than banks. Make personal loans only against money you have in savings. Are excellent places to shop for home mortgage loans.

U. of C.   University of Chicago.

U. of I.   University of Illinois at Chicago Circle.

Circle   Same as above.

NU   Northwestern University, specifically the undergraduate campus in Evanston.

FOOD & DRINK FOIBLES

Chocolate soda   A soda with chocolate syrup and vanilla ice cream. The New York phrase "a black and white" draws a blank here. If you want chocolate ice cream as well as chocolate syrup, order a *double* chocolate soda. If you want a Broadway, ask for a chocolate soda with coffee ice cream.

Coffee   All too likely to be poured automatically with your entrée in almost any Chicago area restaurant at noon —protests about preferring it with or after dessert are usually ignored. In hotel banquet rooms, it may be poured as early as the salad.

A sweet roll   A Danish.

Iced tea   Most restaurants willingly make iced tea—except in winter.

Iced coffee   Ask for it in most short-order spots, and you'll throw the waitress into a spasm.

Pop   Any carbonated soft drink—including cream soda. Soda pop.

Soda   Use this word when you want Scotch and – – – –, otherwise you're likely to get bicarbonate of.

Rye   If by rye you mean a blend, order by brand, otherwise the bartender will say he doesn't have rye—or else he'll pour rye whiskey. If you're from the East, you don't want rye whiskey—you want a blend.

Sucker   A lollipop.

CHAPTER I

WHERE TO LIVE

Water fascinates. Chicago treasured its lakefront, beautified it, created a high-rise city along it that is spectacular.

Chicago's heritage is restlessness—a disdain for the old, a passion for the big new. But from the Depression of the 1930s to the early 1950s, Chicago stagnated. When construction finally began, pent-up demand hatched the wildest sort of building boom. Chicago tore down, ripped out, recklessly filled open space along the lakefront with no concern for density.

The boom exploded into high-rise overdevelopment of the Near North Side. It swept into the Lincoln Park area, with its double appeal of lakefront and lovely old park. It transformed Marine Dr. It destroyed old mansions along the lake from Foster to Devon and erected a wall of high rises in their place.

It jettisoned slums near the lake on the Near South Side and created new racially integrated high rises and town houses in their place. It infilled the lakefront in Hyde Park. It transformed the shoreline in South Shore. In the downtown area, east of Michigan Av. from Randolph St. north to the Chicago River, it's thrusting the massive Illinois Center Development—condominium and rental high rises for 50,000 people, office high rises for 30,000.

You come here from elsewhere, and you need a place to live. The high-rise city along Lake Michigan looks like the total city. It may not occur to you to look beyond. Yet people do. There's a significant trend among bolder young couples and singles to reject high-rise living for old houses in old communities a few miles west of the lakefront. The houses need upgrading and restoration, but because of Chicago's tough building code, they're basically sound. The areas are unpretentious, and the neighbors polyglot. The pioneers gamble on the neighborhoods, and the gamble makes sense. It's a way to own your own home, have a garden, live close in with a sense of community—and not be in the suburbs. With all its problems, all its discomforts, the city gives its citizens a sense of belonging to something beautifully unique.

Integration is spotty, but it exists. The most successfully integrated old-line community in the U.S. is Hyde Park-Kenwood on the South Side. Some middle-income blacks live in essentially white areas. A few affluent blacks own condominium apartments on the Near North Side; a few more rent in high rises there.

The big lacks throughout the city are new homes for moderate-income families and decent housing for the poor. The official city pays lip service to human dignity, but it doesn't create conditions that can lessen indignities. It's a damn shame.

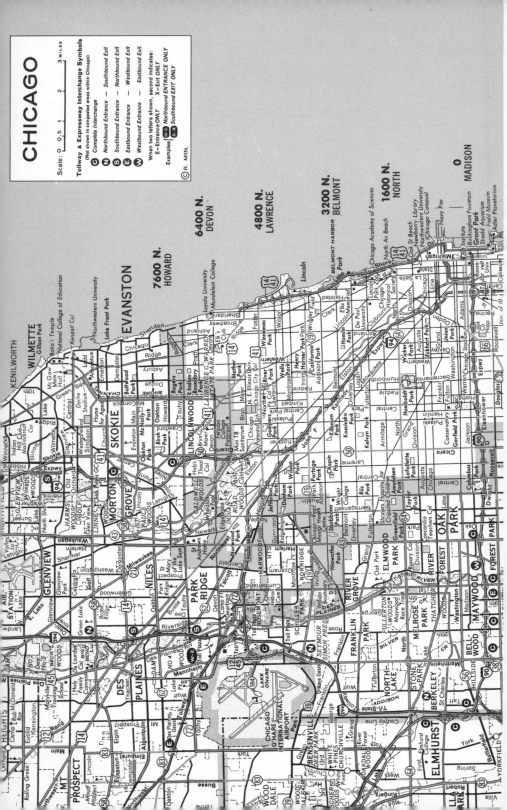

Crime & Neighborhoods. Abrupt contrasts between the haves and have-nots explain much of the crime rate in desirable city neighborhoods—especially housebreaking and burglary,* muggings, car and bike theft. In this city, neighborhoods can change drastically within a block or two. For instance, just two blocks west of complacent Sandburg Village is unadulterated slum.

Yet, often the change works in reverse. In the center of a seedy residential area, you find a pocket of new low-rise condominiums or handsomely maintained old houses or ventures into private renovation. There's more of this than most Chicagoans realize—ignore anyone who tells you that only one or two or even all of the neighborhoods sampled below are the only city neighborhoods worth living in.

Schools. If public schools are your prime concern, you'll probably decide to live in the suburbs. Transferred families with absolutely no time to investigate schools in town really must head out—unless they can afford private or parochial schools. With a little time to make a decision on where to live, read Chapter VII, "Parents' Guide to Schools," and look for housing in neighborhoods where public schools are recommended.

There are so many valid reasons for living in town, for bringing up children in town—the city's open society, its marvelous people mix, its wealth of cultural institutions to be visited and enjoyed, its entertainment spectrum, its medical resources, its shopping resources. The city is dynamic in a way the suburbs can never be.

A SAMPLING OF NEIGHBORHOODS

NORTH

Near North Side. For housing, Chicago River to North Av. (1600 N.), Lake Shore Dr. west to LaSalle St. (150 W.).† Chic, sleek, marvelously convenient. Cosmopolitan mix of high-rise offices and apartments, fashionable shops and restaurants, society churches, prestige hotels, lakefront esplanade, university buildings, medical center, Rush St. night life, singles bars, "Delaware Riviera," and Oak St. Beach. A high-rise kingdom for singles and childless couples. Great sense of independence throughout neighborhood.

Demerits. Expensive. Congested. Frequently overrun with conventioneers and visitors. Lack of privacy in high-rise apartments facing other high-rise apartments. Demand for excessive building security by some tenants a damned nuisance to other tenants and guests.†† Garage space at a premium. Street parking almost impossible.

Housing. Ferocious rentals. At Dewitt Apts., 260 E. Chestnut, for instance, studio $200-250; 1-bedroom $320-400; 2-bed $435-575; 3-bed $580-675; garage $45. At 1000 Lake Shore Plaza, 2-bed $700-950; 3-bed $850-1,875 (duplex); 4-bed $1,425-1,600; garage $53.80. By comparison, at Sandburg

---

* Housebreaking is also a serious problem in the suburbs, though the have-nots there are mainly kids on drugs looking for stuff to fence.

† For street numbering system, see p. 38.

†† A smart professional burglar can still crack any building in this city.

Village, the compound for singles and young couples, studio $185-225; 1-bed $230-310; 2-bed $325-410; self-park garage $32.50-37.50. Town-house rental here (long waiting list) $400-600, depending on size; some artist studios at $300. A 2-bed condominium on Lake Shore Dr. costs $65,000-500,000 and a studio $25,000-50,000. Spacious old town houses command minimum $85,000 on a 20-ft. side-street lot, can easily go to $135,000 on a 25-ft. lot on elegant Astor St.

Lincoln Park. For housing, North Av. to Diversey (2800 N.), Lincoln Park west to Lakewood (1300 W.). Beautiful space along park, superb view to lakefront from high rises overlooking. Tremendous people mix—all ages,* all income levels, all sexes, and in many sections, varied ethnic backgrounds, different races. Wealth only semiapparent; you don't feel compelled to prove your income. Between 1900 and 2400 north, Clark west to Lakewood, rewarding subareas (Park West, DePaul, Sheffield) where young couples who want to raise their children in city buy turn-of-the-century homes, restore or remodel. Good transportation: buses, El, cabs. Some people walk to Loop; hundreds bike down, using lakefront bike path. Interesting small restaurants. Strong independent liberal group and Independent alderman (43rd Ward). Residents politically concerned and activist in local matters. Busy neighborhood conservation organizations raise funds for upgrading and improvements through art fairs, plant and sculpture sales, garden walks, etc.

Demerits. Some old commercial streets deteriorating. No convenient full-service bank. Shops are neighborhood—too many of some kinds (record shops, ma-and-pa grocery stores); too few of others (no elegant shops whatsoever). Street parking usually difficult in residential areas.

Housing. New high rises and town houses, apartment buildings of varying age and quality, private homes, 4+1s.† A 2-bedroom older apartment with full dining room, 2 bathrooms, on good side street $300. Condominiums $35,000-125,000. In new developments in the Lincoln-Larrabee area from North Av. to Webster, town houses $29,000-60,000; rentals with one-year leases at Walpole Point 1-bed $215, 2-bed $275, 3-bed to $360; at fully integrated West Park Place with one-year lease (rentals geared to income requirements, $8,000-12,000), 3-bed town houses $191, 4-bed $220, 3-bed apartments $180. Handsomely rehabilitated old houses on Cleveland and Sedgwick command prices $80,000-95,000, in two recent instances $250,000 each. Prices drop ($28,000-42,000) farther west in DePaul-Sheffield area on streets like Dayton, Fremont, Bissell and beyond El tracks (five minutes to Loop). Dayton 2100 block good example of contemporary heterogeneous city living—one Chinese, one Japanese, one Puerto Rican, one black family, several old German couples (neighborhood was German), and Americans of varied religious backgrounds.

---

* One of the city's highest concentration of ages 25-34 (1:4) is here in the area bounded by Fullerton-Diversey-Clark.

† Five-story elevator buildings, wood construction with brick or stone facades. Ground floor mainly parking. Look expensive, but cheaply made to last no more than 20 years at most. Appeal mainly to singles and young couples who put up with faults for the sake of living in area.

Old Town Area of Lincoln Park. North Av. to Armitage (2000 N.), Clark west to Larrabee (600 W.). Until late 1972, an area mainly of restored old Victorian homes owned by editors, artists, authors, professional people with nice disdain for bland conformity. Now three huge new high rises face Lincoln Park at north end of area.

Demerits. Notable absence of amenities like shoemaker, first-rate drugstore, full-service bank. Wells St. currently so tacky, hippy, tourist trappy, you work to find the few interesting restaurants, jazz/folk spots, unique shops. Wells St. crime rate spills throughout area (muggings, burglaries), goes up and down as do gang problems. Narrow one-way residential streets make it hard to get in. Street parking hopeless, even for residents.

Housing. Some homes or apartments in converted homes for rent. New high rises (Eugenie Square, Americana Towers, Kennelly Square) rent at Sandburg prices or higher. Efficiency and 1-bedroom in old remodeled walk-ups $130-160; in some old buildings, 4-7 rooms $190-300. Restored homes $90,000-125,000. Unrestored $66,000.

Lakeview. For housing, Diversey north to Irving Park (4000 N.), lakefront west toward Clark (Clark angles from 600-1300 W.). Neighborhood along Sheridan Rd. much like adjacent Lincoln Park. Convenient. Good public transportation. Highly mixed streets west of Broadway but sound old buildings; remodeling is upgrading parts of blocks. Young professional couples buy old three-flats, remodel to live in one, rent out other two. Except for New Town (subneighborhood attracting new-style young adults), Lakeview is families and fairly stable. Also characterized by strong liberal element (44th Ward) that elected Independent alderman over incredible machine opposition. As in Lincoln Park, the full-time ward office (p. 137) serves as strong neighborhood catalyst for overall improvements.

Demerits. Neighborhood deteriorates into iffy area north of 3500 Broadway. Also becomes shabby (though private homes) west of Halsted. Northwest section badly deteriorated. Broadway (main New Town drag) noted for proliferation of here-today-gone-tomorrow shops. Girl-hassling along Diversey-Clark-Broadway more gross than on Rush. Street parking impossible except during day. Long side streets west of Broadway not as well lit or safe as single girls could wish.

Housing. High rises and enormous old apartments along Sheridan Rd. Old-fashioned courtyard apartments on side streets. New 4+1s, old two- and three-flats. In Mies van der Rohe high rises at Diversey overlooking Lincoln Park, studio $185-235; 1-bedroom $235-325; 2-bed $325-425; 3- and 4-bed $400-600. Side-street 4+1 studio $140-160; 1- and 2-bed $185-250. In large old Sheridan Rd. elevator buildings, 7- 9-room apartments $675-850. Old 5-room apartments, Broadway area or west, $200-275. Old three-flat to buy/remodel $50,000 up. Condominiums $35,000-65,000.

Marine Dr. Strip of Uptown. For housing, Marine Dr. between Irving Park and Foster (5200 N.). Another neighborhood changing drastically from block to block. Distinguished old high rises, good new ones on Marine Dr., beautiful old homes on a few side streets like Castlewood Terrace, Hutchinson, Hazel,

Junior Terrace, Cullom, but two-three blocks west of Marine Dr., instant calamity to Broadway. West of Broadway, neighborhood improves again, mainly old, single middle-class family homes. What's in between is what most Chicagoans call Uptown—an enclave of poor Appalachians, poor American Indians, poor blacks, poor Latins, hippies, white senior citizens living on Social Security and welfare. City's highest concentration of senior citizens lives here. Neighborhood likely to improve with completion of new Mayfair College—real estate developers have moved in. Meanwhile, shopping only fair at best; restaurants primarily greasy spoon. Good bus transportation.

Housing. Newer Marine Dr. high rises, studio $135-160; 1-bedroom $200-240; 2-bed $287-340. Houses on prestige streets like Hutchinson, Castlewood Terrace $70,000-90,000. Houses (frame or brick) west of Broadway $23,000-35,000. Condominiums $35,000-60,000.

Edgewater Area of Uptown. For housing, Balmoral (5400 N.) to Devon (6400 N.), lakefront west to El tracks. On Sheridan Rd., Edgewater Beach apartments (one superb old tower), new Edgewater Beach complex, and "Miami Beach North"—high-rise apartments, high-rise condominiums from Hollywood to Devon. Streets immediately west, mix of older apartments, walk-ups, 4 + 1s. Loyola University, Mundelein College, Convent of the Sacred Heart spread heavy Roman Catholic influence. East Edgewater one of few areas where you can live close to lake and El.

Demerits. Shopping spotty, only fair at best. Dearth of restaurants, night life. Yet singles, students, young couples attracted by lower rents, proximity of beaches, El. Rash of scruffy nursing and convalescent homes. Sheridan Rd. high rises have effectively walled off from lake the neighborhood to the immediate west. Long CTA bus ride to Loop. El trip from Loop frightening at night. Off-street parking imperative—or eschew car ownership.

Housing. Sheridan Rd. high rises $185-420. Old walk-ups $140-175. In 4 + 1s, studio $140-160; 1-bedroom $185-200. Condominiums $40,000-65,000. Older houses $27,000-50,000.

Rogers Park (commonly called East Rogers Park). For housing, Devon north to city limits, lakefront west to Ridge (angles 1200-1900 W.). Filled with contrasts because of recent tremendous influx of singles, young couples into old, once predominantly Jewish middle-middle-class neighborhood. Community now multiracial, multi-socioeconomic from lakefront west to Ashland. West of Ashland, mainly Jewish and Catholic. Prime attractions: substantially lower rents, new buildings (mostly 4 + 1s), sturdy older homes on nice side streets, and upgrading of older buildings. North Eastlake Terrace, a slightly offbeat little pocket of new, old apartments with beach, lake at back door. Shopping on Devon, Clark, Morse, plus sprinkling of stores on Sheridan Rd. and on Howard.

Demerits. Convenient to Loop only if you're close to El or have a car. On CTA buses, a tedious trip. Few good restaurants and bars. One badly deteriorated little six-block area between Howard and Evanston boundary three blocks west of Sheridan Rd., black and Spanish-speaking. Blacks who fled caved-in Woodlawn on South Side for this section are horrified.

Housing. Four rooms $165 up; 4 or 5 rooms with backyard and parking or terrace and parking $230-250. Eastlake Terrace, 1-bedroom $200 up. Large old houses $25,000-35,000.

West Ridge (commonly called West Rogers Park). For housing, irregular south boundary—Bryn Mawr-Peterson (6000 N.)—to city limits at Howard, west from Ridge to Kedzie (3200 W.). Well-maintained middle-class neighborhood, mainly synagogue-oriented Jewish families and widows (10-12% of community population). Good choice of housing: substantial two-story homes, small ranches, bungalows, two- to six-flat apartment buildings, town houses. Good shopping on Devon and in nearby Lincoln Village. Excellent Jewish community center serves entire neighborhood.

Demerits. Very homogeneous neighborhood in looks as well as spirit because almost all homes of brick, built on 35-ft. lots. Not for young singles— no night life, few good restaurants. Long bus ride to Loop, nearest commuter train (North Western RR) in "East" Rogers Park.

Housing. Nicer homes average $50,000-60,000 near city limits, but homes range from $35,000 to a few at $100,000. Condominium apartments in expensive Winston Towers high rises $28,000-51,800 (3-bedroom). Walk-up apartments in older buildings, 1-bed $140-165; 2-bed $175-200; 3-bed $225-350 In newer elevator buildings, 1-bed $165-185; 2-bed $200-265; 3-bed $350-375.

NORTHWEST

Sauganash Area of Forest Glen. Bryn Mawr (5600 N.) to Devon (city limits here), west from Pulaski (4000 W.) to Cicero (4800 W.). Lily-white urban area laid out like a suburb. Substantial, custom-type homes ($40,000-115,000). Very cohesive place filled with politicos who have to live in city. Entire neighborhood mad for competitive exterior Christmas decorations and effects.

Demerits. No easily accessible public transportation. Nearest shopping, Lincoln Village shopping center, Lincoln at McCormick.

Caldwell Woods-Edgebrook Areas of Forest Glen. West and northwest of Sauganash between Elston, Touhy (7200 N.), Cicero. Pretty area on both sides of North Branch of Chicago River and forest preserves (preserves are woods and meadows held in perpetuity by Cook County for public use). Nice homes tucked into woodsy streets, hidden and visually charming. Middle-class white. Houses in $35,000-70,000 bracket. Wildwood section of Edgebrook north of Devon most woodsy section of all. About 25 min. from Loop via Milwaukee RR commuter trains.

Demerits. Rough motorcycle gangs tear into forest preserves at night— drugs, booze, and several murders of young boys. Nearest shopping center, Lincoln Village.

O'Hare Area. Annexed area west from Cumberland (8400 W.) between Kennedy Expy and East River Rd. (both 8800 W. and 4400 N. here). Growing new high-rise community near O'Hare Airport attracts singles, divorced swingers. Handy to forest preserves, singles bars, jobs at airport, various corporate headquarters and industrial centers in Elk Grove Village, Bensenville. Open space, like cornfields across road. Sense of freedom found in any still-building community. Near Higgins-Cumberland shopping and Harlem-Irving Park shopping center.

Demerits. Little stability. Car imperative. Isolated complex like Lamplighter Towers tries to compensate with what's called total living—pools, health club, social activities. Catherine Courts has its own shopping.

Housing. At developments like Lamplighter, studio $180 up; 1-bedroom $225 up; 2-bed $295 up; two-story 2- and 3-bed $495-742. At Catherine Courts, studio $175 up; 1-bed $215 up; 2-bed $295. Condominiums $30,000-40,000.

WEST

Circle Campus Area of Near West Side. For housing, Harrison (600 S.) to Taylor (1000 S.), west from Morgan (1000 W.) to Ashland (1600 W.). One of least-known enclaves in city; in many ways, one of the most intriguing since community is basically Italo-American and as village-minded as if it were in southern Italy or Sicily. Much life on the streets, clusters of kids. Students, some faculty from Circle Campus and University of Illinois medical school, physicians affiliated with West Side Medical Center have discovered community. Students live in Italian-owned walk-ups; professionals mainly occupy three new town-house developments or buy old homes when available. Blacks live in older Jane Addams project. Mexicans live on fringes of the neighborhood. New shopping center with supermarket and bank. Excellent public transportation—15 min. to Loop via CTA buses, 7 min. by El. Instant access to Eisenhower Expy.

Demerits. Village-minded means working-class Italo-American community is not worldly, is slow to accept you, is occasionally suspicious, often resents students because they bring in black friends, don't live like families, clobber all street parking. Taylor is dividing line between community and black ghetto—hostility reaches across. Only two small restaurants; no night life in area, not even at Circle Campus because it's a commuter university.

Housing. New town-house and mid-rise developments—Circle Square, Campus Green, Westgate. Circle Square two-story town houses ($30,000-60,000), face own green, have patios. Built by developers who were told: "Italian families always want apartment for the mother-in-law." So built Mamma Mia ground-level apartments in $60,000 town houses. Alas, Italians not interested. So town houses may be rented—entire town house $300; Mamma Mia $190. In Circle Square mid-rise, 1-bedroom $175. At Campus Green with pool, garage, studio $182-218; 1-bed $220-270; 2-bed $340-374. Town houses $45,000-50,000.

To buy old house on attractive streets like Bishop, Lexington, ask around. Maybe check with Father Gino Dalpiaz, Our Lady of Pompeii Church. This also good way to find walk-ups. Rents swing wildly, depending on improvements. With none, 2-bed from $80, and it helps to have a little student life-style left in you. With improvements, as 6 rooms with fireplace, patio $275 up.

SOUTH

Near South Side. What Chicagoans call the Near South Side is actually the new interracial section of Douglas. For housing, lakefront west to Prairie (300 E.), 26th to 35th Sts. Distinct high-rise, mid-rise, town-house complexes for approximately 14,000 people in areas reclaimed from urban decay and slums. At Lake Meadows and Prairie Shores, fine open space, dramatic views of lake and Loop. Newer South Commons buildings face in—to courtyards with flowering trees, shrubs, swimming pools, play areas, strollers' malls. Lake Meadows, Prairie Shores totally integrated, relaxed about it. People who move here (many professionals) have faced facts, choose to live here for variety of reasons—the experience itself, closeness to Loop (10-15 min. by bus), good housing for relatively low rents, proximity to their work areas (the Loop; Mercy and Michael Reese Hospitals; R.R. Donnelley, the printers; Illinois Institute of Technology). All complexes have shopping centers, some sports facilities.

Demerits. Feeling of living in compounds with hostile territory at periphery. Everything done within compound. Nearest outside restaurants in or near Chinatown—22nd at Wentworth. Public transportation fine, but if you rely on the El, you have to walk through bleak areas to get to your compound. Helps greatly to have car. Tenants at South Commons so economically and socially diverse (low income and middle class) they don't homogenize.

Housing. In Lake Meadows, studio to 3-bedroom $110-275; luxury building apartments $145-440. In Prairie Shores, studio to 3-bed $95-273. In South Commons, studio to 2-bed $137-300; 3-bed duplex $425; town houses, $51,000-53,000.

Hyde Park-Kenwood. For housing, lakefront west to Cottage Grove, 47th to 59th Sts. Hyde Park-Kenwood is its own world. People who live here wouldn't live elsewhere. University of Chicago presence dominates all with international cast: faculty, staff, students, grad students—emphasis on abstract intellectuality. Intellectuals especially attracted to vitality of black life-style— hence success of integration in much of area.* Great individuality, sense of freedom. Emphatic community organization, sometimes frantically activist. Outspoken Independent alderman (5th Ward), full-time ward office. Marvelous housing mix—fine old homes with huge lawns, town houses old and new,† yet 85% of area old Chicago-style walk-ups. Community trying to preserve low-rise character. Excellent shopping center and shopping strips— 53rd, 55th, 57th Sts. First-rate transportation—15 min. to Loop via IC trains. Also CTA buses. Jackson Park, Museum of Science & Industry part of neighborhood.

---

*Where Near South Side is recent planned integration, Hyde Park-Kenwood developed naturally in basically fine, old, but deteriorating neighborhood. Massive land clearance, rehabilitation, building boom with plan behind new construction created present neighborhood. It is the only area in city where white population increased between 1960 and 1970.

† Harper Square, the most socially experimental high rise in U.S., is here. Built by Amalgamated Clothing Workers as part of social program, it integrates professional, blue-collar, and low-income families of varied races in quality apartments that are undifferentiated by income level. On surface, a co-op, but if you want to move out, you get your money back.

Demerits. Deliberate Bohemianism and Hyde Park masochism (I-needn't-look-pretty-because-I'm-smart) sometimes hard to accept. Young swingers lost here. Not enough restaurants, no night life (though University overwhelms with cultural events for community-at-large). Crime a problem (desperate black poverty immediately north and south of area) but coming under control with tight security system.

Housing. Tight. Vacancy rate so low (one-half of 1%) that except in some new high rises you really have to hunt. Studio in old walk-ups $100-135; 1-bedroom $150-160; 2-bed $175-200; 3-bed $200-250. In high rises, efficiency $165-200; 1-bed $240 up; 2-bed $295 up; 3-bed $400 up. Houses $38,000-100,000 plus. Condominiums $25,000-55,000.

South Shore. 67th to 79th Sts., lakefront west to Stony Island Av. (1600 E.). Good example of what happens to a fine neighborhood when whites flee as blacks move in—schools change because of breakdown of institutional support, shops close, the power base erodes. Not a Hyde Park-Kenwood, though determined core of integrated liberals trying mightily to achieve in east section. Biggest concentration of whites on South Shore Dr., south of 71st, east of Exchange. Jackson Highlands (67th to 71st Sts., Jeffery west to Cregier), distinguished upper-middle-class black enclave. Rents stabilized. Fine homes at bargain prices attract both races despite high taxes. Shopping on 71st, 75th, 79th. Few restaurants. Night life in black-owned integrated nightclubs on shopping streets. Fast IC trains to Loop, 25 min.

Demerits. Little feeling of neighborhood settling down. Not helped by boarded stores and homes (boarded to satisfy city ordinance against unoccupied structures). Neighborhood declines badly near Stony Island, welfare recipients moving in. Random violence, armed robbery in much of area.

Housing. In old walk-ups, efficiencies $100; 3 rooms $124-135; 4 rooms $150. In newer buildings, add $25 across board. Fine large houses, 30-40 years old, $30,000-75,000—in good suburban areas, they'd go at twice the price. Condominiums $25,000-35,000.

Park Manor (Greater Grand Crossing). 71st to 79th Sts., King Dr. (400 E.) to Dan Ryan Expy (200 W.). Long-established, black middle-class community with roots in early 1920s. One of best-maintained communities in Chicago: single-family homes, two-story brick flats, several new medical centers. Same shopping streets South Shore uses, same restaurants, nightclubs. Low crime rate. Dan Ryan Rapid Transit to Loop, 15 min.

Demerits. Scarcity of available homes for newcomers—little turnover in older homes, little new building. Limited shopping along East 71st because of flight of white merchants.

Housing. One-bedroom $125; 2-bed $145. Homes $25,000-40,000.

Marynook (Avalon Park). 83rd to 87th Sts., Dorchester (1400 E.) to IC tracks. Mainly black (10-15% white) community with enough bi-levels, tri-levels, two-story homes built 1955-56 to be attractive to younger middle-class couples. Homes set on curved streets around Avalon Park, no alleys. Relatively low crime rate, less anxiety about crime than in Hyde Park. Good transportation to Loop: Dan Ryan Rapid Transit 20 min., IC trains 30 min. Shopping on 87th. Night life, restaurants on 75th, 79th, 87th.

Demerits. Apathy toward community organization. Pressures from low-income families squeezing into other sections of Avalon Park—for instance, residents don't feel free to walk neighborhood at night or go into park. No grocery store within walking distance.

Housing. Homes $22,000-35,000, occasionally come on market as rentals.

FAR SOUTH

Pill Hill (Calumet Heights). 90th to 93rd Sts., Jeffery (2000 E.) to about Stony Island. Name comes from concentration of white physicians living in area ten years ago. Some still here along with other whites, but Pill Hill mainly a prestige black community. Houses on hill view distant Loop. Substantial homes. Ranches, bi-levels, tri-levels, mainly $45,000-65,000 but some to $150,000. Low crime rate. IC trains to Loop. Shopping at 87th & Commercial, 95th & Jeffery. Also Evergreen Plaza Shopping Center, 95th & Western; larger River Oaks Shopping Center, Calumet City, about half-hour drive.

Beverly Hills-Morgan Park. 87th to 119th Sts., approximately Vincennes to Western (2400 W.). Two communities that often see themselves as one. Small-town quality in beautiful terrain—quiet, sedate, liquorless, firm sense of roots, history. Big on community spirit, especially proud of public schools. Largely white middle-class Irish-Catholic, balance Protestant and Jewish (one Jewish congregation). Beverly Hills beginning to accept blacks on semi-integrated basis. Morgan Park's black community established years ago but not integrated. On dollar-for-dollar basis, best place in Chicago to look for homes: $45,000-50,000 for house commanding $90,000 in Winnetka. Good homes as low as $25,000. Good transportation: 35-45 min. to Loop via Rock Island commuter trains or Dan Ryan. Evergreen Plaza Shopping Center plus small scattered shopping areas. Beverly Art Center, Drury Lane Theatre help fill cultural void.

Demerits. Conformist and sometimes bigoted. Few restaurants. No night life.

Pullman. For housing in South Pullman Historic District, 111th to 115th Sts., Langley (700 E.) to Cottage Grove. Famous as first wholly planned 19th-century urban town. (Architect Solon Beman designed all for Pullman Car Co.) Factories, offices, man-made lake long gone; arcade, park, church, sturdy small brick row houses, larger unattached homes remain. Blue-collar neighborhood discovered in past ten years by young architects, urban planners, artists, grad students. Tremendous sense of history, community, zest for restoration. One of lowest crime rates in city. IC commuter trains 20 min. to Loop, 12 min. to University of Chicago. CTA bus links to Dan Ryan Rapid Transit—30 min. total to Loop. Car helpful. Excellent River Oaks Shopping Center about half hour away.

Demerits. Surrounded by industry, hence island feeling. Few homes large enough for large families. Typical row house small by contemporary standards. Close to some of worst pollution in U.S., but because of prevailing winds, upwind most of time.

Housing. Big differences here because of sizes, degree of restoration. Apartments $50-225. Rented house $120-300. Purchase $12,000-30,000.

THE SUBURBS

Chicago's suburbs are so varied that you can come here as a transferee and match what you've left. You can find old communities with spacious homes, tree-lined streets, sense of Establishment, and deep roots. You can find new developments built around man-made lakes, putting green, community clubhouse, and swimming pool. Anything that exists elsewhere is here— suburban complexes for singles and young couples, blue-collar suburbs, status suburbs, integrated suburbs, ethnic suburbs, town-house and con- dominium suburbs, tract developments, horse-country suburbs, close-in suburbs, far-out suburbs, even a handful of suburbs in rolling terrain. Con- fronted by more than 250 suburbs spread over six counties (plus two in In- diana), where—and how—do you find the one that's right for you?

Begin with the table on the next page, *Status Ranking of 200 Suburbs.*

Economic tables can be a drag, but this one gives you a practical way to cull suburbs. Look for those in which the educational backgrounds of the adults and the median family income are similar to yours. Spot them on a map. They'll tend to cluster in various locations—north, northwest, west, etc. These are your starting points. Choose your direction and start exploring.

Old vs. New. Some old Chicago suburbs are quite beautiful. By contrast most new suburbs look awfully raw and exposed. But aside from their air of being well-established, older communities are desirable because their taxes are stable. Schools, sewers, streets, street lights, adequate police and fire protection were paid for long ago. In growing new developments, these needs are constantly being enlarged; so are the tax assessments that support them.

Old suburbs have well-established cultural lives—active symphony orchestras, art centers, and historical societies. New developments try hard to generate a sense of community with planned recreational activities, but the lack of enriching opportunities is felt. Old suburbs have their own shopping and/or business district; new developments may be miles from the nearest stores. Old suburbs have a greater people mix; new suburbs are essentially one-class white. The newest suburbs are likely to be filled with young families so exclusively that needs like baby-sitters go unmet.

Families that rush to the new developments miles from Chicago do so, not just because home prices are lower, but because they think they'll get more house for their money—an extra bedroom perhaps. They like the sense of unrestricted space—just open the door, let the kids out to play. They anticipate the exhilaration of pioneering in a new community.

What they don't realize is that the extra bedroom exists because all the rooms are smaller than in an older house; that the touted fireplace and air-conditioning are never included in the advertised price; that the extras nonexistent in older communities—swimming pool, sauna, free bus to commuter station—scarcely offset the disadvantages of having to conform to an incredible number of development regulations.

Worst of all, new housing, for the most part, has been constructed as cheaply as possible. It may be hideously defective, may have been built on floodplain, may, as at Hanover Park, have been built next to a concealed

Continued on p. 28

STATUS RANKING OF 200 SUBURBS*

Rank†	Municipality	College Graduates (25 or older) %	Rank	Families with Incomes of $25,000 or More %	Rank	Median Family Income Dollars	Rank	Median Years of School (25 or older) Years	Rank
1	Kenilworth	58.1	1	62.1	1	$34,573	1	16.2	1
2	Winnetka	53.9	2	55.3	4	28,782	4	15.9	4
3	Glencoe	46.9	5	55.9	3	29,565	3	15.4	5
4	Olympia Fields	43.2	7	58.2	2	29,781	2	15.1	6
5	Lincolnshire	50.0	3	41.9	9	22,984	8	16.0	2.5
6	Barrington Hills	42.5	8	52.6	5	27,647	5	15.0	7.5
7	Flossmoor	40.9	10	50.0	6	24,898	7	14.7	10.5
8	Wilmette	44.2	6	39.8	11	21,809	10	15.0	7.5
9	Lake Bluff	49.7	4	32.4	15	19,967	17	16.0	2.5
10	Lake Forest	39.7	12	43.8	8	22,686	9	14.7	10.5
11	Northfield	40.0	11	37.8	13	21,268	12	14.6	12
12	Deerfield	41.2	9	30.8	16	20,050	15	14.8	9
13	River Forest	35.9	16.5	40.6	10	21,236	13	14.2	17
14	Highland Park	37.0	15	37.2	14	20,749	14	14.4	15
15	Oak Brook	32.0	23	49.8	7	24,923	6	13.3	25
16	Northbrook	37.3	13	30.5	18	19,994	16	14.5	13.5
17	Hinsdale	37.1	14	30.7	17	19,185	19	14.5	13.5
18	Western Springs	35.9	17.5	28.7	20	19,502	18	14.3	16
19	Glenview	32.8	22	29.6	19	19,137	20	14.0	19.5
20	Lincolnwood	24.9	32	37.9	12	21,365	11	13.2	28.5
21	Glen Ellyn	34.8	18	18.4	28	17,680	22	14.1	18
22	Clarendon Hills	33.1	20	18.5	27	17,635	23	13.7	23
23	Naperville	32.9	21	14.7	35	16,818	27	14.0	19.5
24	La Grange	28.5	26	18.0	29	16,552	28	13.3	25
25	Riverside	26.8	27	19.5	25.5	16,389	32	13.3	25
26	Park Ridge	23.6	36.5	20.5	24	17,472	24	13.0	31.5
27	Barrington	28.0	30.5	21.0	22	16,311	33	12.9	34
28	Wheaton	32.0	24	14.2	37	15,055	40	13.8	21.5
29	Arlington Heights	28.0	30.5	14.8	34	17,034	26	12.9	34
30	Palatine	25.2	29	11.5	43	16,072	34	13.2	28.5
31	Skokie	20.6	43.5	19.5	25.5	16,423	31	12.8	38
32	Palos Park	19.6	45	27.1	21	18,762	21	12.6	52
33	Evanston	33.7	19	16.1	30	13,932	62	13.2	28.5
34	Homewood	23.7	35	13.9	39	15,758	36	13.0	31.5
35	Mount Prospect	21.0	42	14.0	38	16,503	29	12.9	34
36	La Grange Park	23.6	36.5	15.0	33	15,237	38	12.8	38
37	Palos Heights	16.9	52	20.7	23	17,082	25	12.6	52
38	Winfield	25.3	28	10.0	47.5	15,385	37	12.7	43.5
39	Libertyville	24.7	33	14.3	36	14,560	44	12.7	43.5
40	Elmhurst	21.3	41	15.1	32	14,955	41.5	12.7	43.5
41	Downers Grove	23.3	38	10.6	45	14,524	46	12.8	38
42	Park Forest	30.2	25	8.0	62.5	13,951	61	13.8	21.5
43	Munster	20.6	43.5	13.2	40	15,108	39	12.6	52
44	Morton Grove	14.4	65.5	15.2	31	16,488	30	12.6	52
45	Oak Park	24.6	35	12.8	41	13,823	67	12.8	38
46	Buffalo Grove	22.9	40	5.6	83.5	14,833	43	13.2	28.5
47	Westchester	13.7	69	11.1	44	15,812	35	12.5	64
48	Itasca	15.5	59	11.7	42	14,432	48	12.5	64
49	Elk Grove Village	18.2	48	6.1	76	14,155	52	12.7	43.5
50	Glenwood	14.8	61	8.2	60.5	14,429	49	12.6	52
51	Hoffman Estates	17.7	50	5.4	86.5	14,549	45	12.7	43.5
52	Lombard	15.8	58	7.2	68.5	14,087	55	12.6	52
53	Hazel Crest	16.2	55	5.8	80	14,101	54	12.6	52
54	Lisle	16.4	54	6.4	73	14,107	53	12.5	64
55	Geneva	17.5	51	9.9	49	13,217	83	12.5	64
56	Crystal Lake	17.8	49	7.9	64.5	13,734	71	12.5	64
57	Matteson	13.4	70	8.0	62.5	14,045	59	12.5	64
58	Des Plaines	12.7	74.5	7.6	67	14,056	58	12.5	64
59	Country Club Hills	12.9	73	7.1	70	14,058	57	12.5	64
60	Bloomingdale	12.7	74.5	8.5	56.5	13,422	74	12.5	64
61	Roselle	11.2	84	8.7	54.5	14,190	50	12.4	82
62	Niles	11.7	79.5	8.4	58.5	14,159	51	12.4	82
63	South Holland	10.8	90	9.0	52.5	14,495	47	12.4	82
64	Woodridge	19.9	43	3.7	128.5	13,870	65	12.7	43.5
65	Rolling Meadows	14.7	62.5	5.2	90	13,343	78	12.6	52
66	Orland Park	12.3	77	8.7	54.5	13,741	70	12.4	82
67	Countryside	16.0	56.5	9.5	51	12,976	94	12.4	82
68	Grayslake	13.8	68	8.5	56.5	13,089	87	12.4	82

* Socioeconomic Characteristics and Rankings of Suburban Municipalities of 2,500 or More Persons. By Pierre de Vise, Project Director, Chicago Regional Hospital Study, August 1972. Based on 1970 Census of Population.
† Composite Socioeconomic Rank.

STATUS RANKING OF 200 SUBURBS* (Continued)

Rank†	Municipality	College Graduates (25 or older) %	Rank	Families with Incomes of $25,000 or More %	Rank	Median Family Income Dollars	Rank	Median Years of School (25 or older) Years	Rank
69	St. Charles	13.3	71.5	7.7	66	$13,094	86	12.4	82
70	Villa Park	11.9	78	6.3	74.5	13,616	73	12.4	82
71	Crete	14.4	65.5	10.3	46	12,905	97	12.3	101
72	Schaumburg	16.0	56.5	3.4	138.5	13,888	64	12.6	52
73	Mundelein	14.6	64	4.8	99	13,811	68	12.4	82
74	Carol Stream	22.8	40	3.0	150	13,113	85	12.8	38
75	Lake Zurich	10.5	94	8.2	60.5	13,345	77	12.4	82
76	Wheeling	11.7	79.5	4.6	106.5	13,398	75	12.5	64
77	West Dundee	14.7	62.5	7.2	68.5	12,628	113	12.4	82
78	Oak Lawn	9.6	107.5	8.4	58.5	13,824	66	12.3	101
79	Algonquin	16.8	53	5.0	93	12,760	107	12.4	82
80	Evergreen Park	9.7	106	10.0	47.5	13,903	63	12.2	122
81	Valparaiso	19.2	47	5.9	78	11,580	163	12.6	52
82	Gurnee	12.4	76	4.5	109.5	13,309	79	12.4	82
83	Hickory Hills	11.0	86	4.7	102	12,779	105	12.5	64
84	Bartlett	11.3	81.5	5.2	91	13,088	88	12.3	101
85	Crown Point	13.9	67	4.9	96.5	12,181	134	12.4	82
86	Oak Forest	10.3	97.5	3.8	124	12,949	95	12.5	64
87	Hillside	7.5	132.5	6.8	72	14,079	56	12.2	122
88	Highland	9.9	103.5	5.0	93	12,773	106	12.4	82
89	Rosemont	9.9	103.5	4.9	96.5	12,824	103	12.4	82
90	East Dundee	11.0	86	9.0	52.5	12,466	125	12.2	122
91	Lansing	8.6	121	6.3	74.5	13,069	90	12.3	101
92	Brookfield	9.4	110	5.6	83.5	12,993	93	12.3	101
93	Cary	15.0	60	2.7	162	13,078	89	12.4	82
94	Addison	9.0	116.5	3.9	119	13,303	80	12.4	82
95	Bensenville	8.9	118	5.6	83.5	13,374	76	12.2	122
96	Elgin	8.6	121	5.0	93	11,555	41.5	12.1	145
97	Plainfield	10.2	100	9.8	50	11,912	149.5	12.3	101
98	West Chicago	10.3	97.5	4.6	106.5	12,886	99.5	12.3	101
99	Wood Dale	6.6	143	7.0	71	13,806	69	12.2	122
100	Willow Springs	9.8	105	5.4	86.5	12,713	109	12.2	122
101	Elmwood Park	7.9	128.5	7.9	64.5	13,028	91	12.1	145
102	North Aurora	13.3	71.5	2.6	166.5	12,250	130	12.5	64
103	Dolton	7.4	135	4.1	115.5	13,282	81	12.3	101
104	Alsip	9.0	116.5	3.8	124	12,687	111	12.4	82
105	Griffith	11.6	81	3.3	142	12,308	129	12.4	82
106	Palos Hills	10.5	94	4.4	112	12,580	114	12.2	122
107	Lindenhurst	9.4	110	3.5	136	12,886	99.5	12.3	101
108	Broadview	10.2	100	3.6	132	12,553	117	12.3	101
109	North Riverside	8.2	125	3.8	124	13,219	82	12.2	122
110	Schererville	8.1	126	5.8	80	12,388	126	12.2	122
111	Riverdale	9.3	112.5	3.7	128.5	12,520	119	12.3	101
112	Richton Park	7.0	138.5	3.0	151	12,754	108	12.5	64
113	Hanover Park	7.7	130	2.8	156.5	12,902	98	12.4	82
114	Berkeley	5.3	159.5	4.3	114	13,708	72	12.2	122
115	Waukegan	11.3	82.5	4.7	102	11,478	167	12.2	122
116	Norridge	4.8	168	4.6	106.5	13,996	60	12.1	145
117	Tinley Park	7.6	131	3.2	145.5	12,798	104	12.3	101
118	Glendale Heights	6.9	140	3.1	149.5	12,927	96	12.3	101
119	Batavia	9.1	115	3.9	119	11,808	157	12.3	101
120	Westmont	10.9	88.5	2.4	171.5	12,674	112	12.2	122
121	Marengo	10.6	91.5	4.7	102	10,974	181	12.2	122
122	New Lenox	11.0	86	2.3	175	12,170	135	12.3	101
123	Harwood Heights	5.4	157.5	5.2	90	13,208	84	11.9	168
124	Lockport	8.8	119	3.8	124	12,039	142	12.2	122
125	Hobart	7.5	132.5	4.4	112	12,052	140	12.2	122
126	Franklin Park	5.0	164.5	4.7	102	12,833	102	12.1	145
127	Wauconda	7.0	138.5	4.6	106.5	12,358	127	12.1	145
128	Melrose Park	6.4	143.5	6.0	77	12,121	136	12.0	160.5
129	Warrenville	5.6	155.5	3.4	139.5	12,860	101	12.2	122
130	Chesterton	10.5	94	3.0	151	11,249	173	12.3	101
131	Aurora	9.4	110	4.9	96.5	11,274	170	12.1	145
132	River Grove	7.8	129	3.7	128.5	12,480	124	12.1	145
133	McHenry	9.6	107.5	4.5	109.5	11,912	149.5	12.1	160.5
134	Joliet	9.3	112.5	5.8	80	11,233	174	12.0	160.5
135	Wilmington	6.0	149	4.9	96.5	12,119	137	12.1	145
136	Woodstock	10.6	91.5	2.8	156.5	11,636	161	12.2	122

---

* Socioeconomic Characteristics and Rankings of Suburban Municipalities of 2,500 or More Persons. By Pierre de Vise, Project Director, Chicago Regional Hospital Study, August 1972. Based on 1970 Census of Population.
† Composite Socioeconomic Rank.

STATUS RANKING OF 200 SUBURBS* (Continued)

Rank†	Municipality	College Graduates (25 or older) %	Rank	Families with Incomes of $25,000 or More %	Rank	Median Family Income Dollars	Rank	Median Years of School (25 or older) Years	Rank
137	Maywood	10.0	102	3.9	119	$11,573	164	12.1	145
138	Worth	6.2	146.5	3.3	142	12,514	120	12.2	122
139	Antioch	8.3	124	5.3	88	11,060	179	12.1	145
140	Streamwood	6.2	146.5	1.6	189	12,481	123	12.4	82
141	Schiller Park	6.4	143.5	2.6	166.5	12,695	110	12.2	122
142	Harvard	10.4	96	3.8	124	11,096	177	12.1	145
143	Bellwood	4.9	166.5	3.6	132	13,008	92	12.0	160.5
144	Lowell	7.3	135.5	5.6	83.5	10,437	188	12.1	145
145	Thornton	4.4	172.5	4.7	102	11,656	160	12.2	122
146	Midlothian	5.7	153.5	2.7	162	12,348	128	12.2	122
147	Forest Park	10.2	100	2.7	162	11,941	148	12.0	160.5
148	Highwood	10.9	88.5	3.2	145.5	11,091	178	12.0	160.5
149	North Lake	5.0	164.5	3.9	119	12,561	116	11.8	173
150	Justice	9.2	114	2.0	184	11,745	159	12.2	122
151	Chicago Heights	8.5	123	4.1	115.5	11,153	175	11.9	168
152	Calumet Park	3.2	185.5	3.9	119	12,546	118	12.0	160.5
153	Dyer	5.9	151	2.2	178.5	12,192	133	12.2	122
154	Berwyn	5.9	151	4.4	112	11,836	155	11.5	181
155	Lemont	8.6	121	2.9	153.5	11,503	166	12.0	160.5
156	Blue Island	7.1	137	3.5	136	11,470	168	12.0	160.5
157	Calumet City	5.2	161	3.2	145.5	11,823	156	12.1	145
158	Markham	5.4	157.5	3.5	136	12,045	141	11.8	173
159	South Elgin	4.9	166.5	3.1	148.5	11,846	154	12.1	145
160	Burbank	3.5	184	3.5	137	12,511	121	11.8	173
161	Lake in the Hills	5.9	151	1.8	187	12,237	132	12.1	145
162	Portage	4.5	171	2.9	153.5	11,910	151.5	12.1	145
163	Montgomery	4.3	174.5	3.5	136	11,968	145	11.9	168
164	Romeoville	4.7	169.5	2.4	171.5	12,565	115	11.9	168
165	Porter	6.3	145	2.4	171.5	11,559	165	12.1	145
166	Bolingbrook	4.2	177	1.5	191	12,070	138	12.2	122
167	Stone Park	4.3	174.5	3.7	128.5	12,013	143	11.0	185.5
168	Lyons	6.1	148	2.7	162	11,998	144	11.6	178
169	Crestwood	5.3	159.5	1.4	192.5	11,750	158	12.2	122
170	Winthrop Harbor	4.0	180.5	3.2	145.5	11,963	146	12.0	160.5
171	Chicago Ridge	4.1	179	2.7	162	11,957	147	12.1	145
172	Carpentersville	4.2	177	1.2	195	12,491	122	12.1	145
173	Harvey	5.1	162.5	3.6	132	11,035	180	11.7	176.5
174	North Chicago	7.9	127.5	2.1	181.5	8,899	198	12.1	145
175	Stickney	3.8	182	2.7	162	12,060	139	11.5	181
176	Hometown	4.2	177	0.8	197	11,118	176	12.2	122
177	Hammond	5.1	162.5	2.8	156.5	10,899	184	11.8	173
178	Bridgeview	2.7	190.5	2.2	178.5	11,910	151.5	12.0	160.5
179	Sauk Village	2.3	194	1.9	186	12,245	131	11.7	176.5
180	Gary	5.6	155.5	2.8	156.5	9,819	195	10.9	186.5
181	Zion	5.7	153.5	2.2	178.5	10,302	191	11.8	173
182	Park City	7.3	135.5	0	200	9,821	194	11.9	168
183	Whiting	6.8	141	1.6	189	10,370	190	11.5	181
184	Crest Hill	4.4	172.5	2.0	184	11,611	162	11.3	184
185	Cicero	4.0	180.5	2.7	162	11,265	171	10.7	190
186	South Chicago Heights	2.5	193	3.3	142	10,970	182	10.8	188
187	Burnham	2.7	190.5	2.4	171.5	11,262	172	11.5	181
188	Fox Lake	3.2	185.5	2.3	175	10,704	186	11.5	181
189	Round Lake Park	2.0	195	2.1	181.5	11,381	169	10.9	187.5
190	Cedar Lake	4.7	169.5	1.0	195	10,414	189	11.0	185.5
191	Posen	1.6	197	1.0	195	11,866	153	10.4	196
192	East Chicago	3.6	183	2.5	167.5	9,208	197	9.9	198
193	Dixmoor	1.7	196	2.3	175	10,565	187	10.7	191
194	East Gary	1.3	199	2.5	167.5	10,249	193	10.7	191
195	Steger	2.6	192	2.0	184	10,936	183	10.6	193
196	Summit	3.1	187	2.2	178.5	10,281	192	10.3	197
197	Round Lake Beach	1.4	198	1.4	192.5	10,723	185	10.5	194.5
198	Phoenix	2.8	188.5	0.6	199	9,800	196	10.5	194.5
199	Robbins	2.8	188.5	1.0	196	8,192	199	9.6	199.5
200	East Chicago Heights	0.9	200	1.6	190	8,169	200	9.6	199.5
	Chicago	8.1		4.4		10,242		11.2	
	Suburbs	15.2		9.9		13,380		12.4	

* Socioeconomic Characteristics and Rankings of Suburban Municipalities of 2,500 or More Persons. By Pierre de Vise, Project Director, Chicago Regional Hospital Study, August 1972. Based on 1970 Census of Population.
† Composite Socioeconomic Rank.

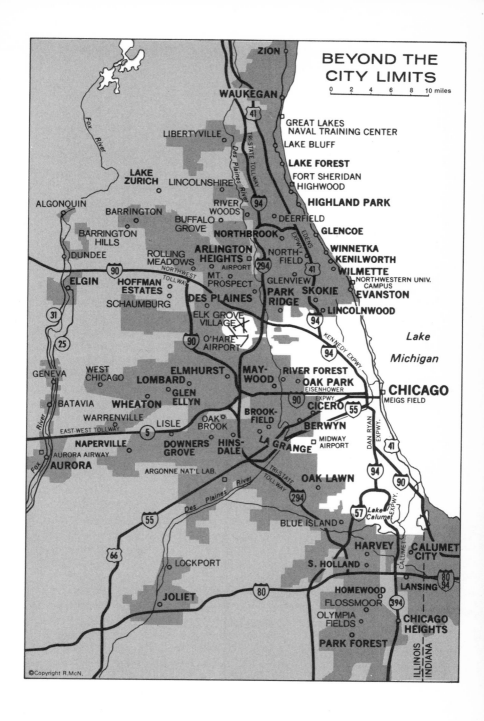

garbage dump—the woes families encounter in new developments are endless.

Commuting. Chicago's suburbs may well be the only suburbs in America where you don't need a second car. The train commuting system here is so superior that there's no reason to get into the hassle of rush hour auto traffic. Commuter trains are new, clean, fast, warm in winter, pleasant in summer—and they run on time.

Finding a House in Four Days. If you're a transferee and this is all the time you have, how do you manage? Obviously, you work with a real estate broker (p. 29). Try to find an old house or at least a house that's been lived in.

An old house in a Chicago suburb could be 100 years old or 80 years old or 20-40 years old. At 100 years it's a status symbol; at 80 years it's about to become one; at 20-40 years it's almost certain to be a better buy than anything newer. It may need a new kitchen and new bathrooms; it may need new wiring or plumbing or a new heating system; you'll have to go through it with an architect (p. 35); but if it's as substantial as it seems and the price is right, take it. If the suburb it's in proves less than enchanting, you can put the house up for sale and get out. Even if it's in a suburb right under one of the two major landing patterns for O'Hare Airport (northwest to southeast and southeast to northwest), you'll sell it.* This is a fast-moving real estate market, and you'll be all right.

Continental Illinois Bank, 231 S. LaSalle, has pulled together some fast-reading area studies on the six counties that contain Chicago's suburbs: Cook, Lake, Du Page, Kane, McHenry, and Will. Each study gives a bit of area history and a map showing the larger suburbs within the area. Suburbs aren't detailed individually beyond new residential construction and community services, but the studies give a useful overview of the county's population characteristics, employment, and industry. Free from the Director of Area Development.

Chicagoland's Community Guide is an annual guide to what its editors call "quality living areas." The guide is probably useful for those facts it does supply about suburbs—prices of homes and town houses, apartment and town-house rentals. However, the guide carefully avoids any racial statistics, thus giving the impression that all Chicago neighborhoods and suburbs are 100% white. It's the kind of omission that leads blacks to feel there's no place in suburbia for them and confirms bigotry in bigots.

FINDING AN APARTMENT, A CONDOMINIUM, OR A HOUSE

You have these options and should use all because desirable places go fast:

1. Classified Ads.† *Chicago Tribune* and *Chicago Sun-Times* carry largest num-

---

* Northwest suburbs subject to nerve-racking noise from 747s and other heavy aircraft: northwest Palatine, Rolling Meadows, some sections of Arlington Heights, Mount Prospect, Des Plaines, Elk Grove Village. Southwest suburbs: Schiller Park, Rosemont, Franklin Park, River Grove.

† See also "Media," p. 52.

ber of ads. Wise to buy Sunday editions Saturday afternoon, look through, phone for Sunday appointments. *Tribune* essential but maddening because it refuses to break down columns of rental ads by area or neighborhood. In the *Trib*, "Apartments North" can mean anywhere from the Chicago River to Evanston. Neighborhood newspapers like *North Loop News, Near North News, Hyde Park Herald* also good bets. Find in neighborhood shops, Laundromats, high-rise lobbies. If you live student life-style, get university papers or *Reader* at campus bookstores.

2. Real Estate Agents. Another annoyance—in *Yellow Pages B* no separation of industrial brokers from residential brokers—but it's all you've got to work with, so plow through. Begin with large firms that have branch offices and a downtown central office because they're obviously not fly-by-night individuals operating out of their apartments. Here are the old Chicago standbys. All handle apartments, houses, condominiums except where noted.

Baird & Warner: Across city and suburbs

Browne & Storch: Near North Side and Hyde Park-Kenwood

Draper & Kramer: Across city and suburbs

E.J. Feulner: Near North Side (not big but reliable, apartments and condominiums only)

Hogan & Farwell: Across city

Kennedy, Ryan, Monigal: Hyde Park-Kenwood

Lake Shore Management: Near North Side (apartments only)

McKey & Poague: Hyde Park-Kenwood, South Shore, Edgewater, south and west suburbs

Monticello Realty: Near North Side, Lakeview (apartments only)

Arthur Rubloff: Near North Side (reliable with qualifications—see p. 33)

Seay & Thomas: Near North Side, Lincoln Park, Lakeview, northwest suburbs (apartments, condominiums only)

Sudler & Co.: Near North Side

Supera: Near North Side, Lincoln Park (mainly remodeled brownstones, renovations)

Wirtz Corp.: North Lake Shore Dr. (apartments only)

These firms manage buildings as well as anyone, and a few, like Monticello, are outstanding. Their leases may be outrageous, but they care about building maintenance, they provide services, and they're discovering that friendly, concerned resident managers and agents make sense.

Suburban equivalents of the above:

Quinlan & Tyson: North Shore, far north and northwest suburbs. Main office, Evanston

Thorsen: North Shore and west suburbs. Main office, LaGrange

Rich Port: West and northwest suburbs. Main office, Park Ridge

Note: If you're a black who wants to explore possibilities outside of black neighborhoods, go to one of the firms above, say that you want to rent. You may be refused—you may not. The incidences of name firms refusing to rent to blacks is decreasing each year—slowly. If you have trouble, call the Chicago Commission on Human Relations, 744-4100, or Leadership Council for Open Communities, 236-9850, or Home Investments Fund (p. 36).

The advantage in working with white realtors is that they handle so much of the desirable real estate. With black realtors you've the chance of better or more personal services, frankness, willingness to go into a black neighborhood at 8 PM to show an apartment or house. For starters try:

Oscar C. Brown Real Estate,   Albert H. Johnson, 732 E. 75th
4649 S. Cottage Grove   Travis Realty Co., 840 E. 87th
Riley-Browne, Inc., 658 E. 63rd

3. Explore on Your Own. Walk, drive, bike around a neighborhood. Small old apartment buildings, walk-ups, 4+1s glue "For Rent" signs showing availabilities on front doors. If a building looks interesting but shows no vacancy sign, find the management office or the janitor or the engineer—ask what's likely to become available. In many buildings, the engineer's name is listed at the buzzers to apartments.

4. Ask people in immediate area for names of local organizations; check with them. Neighborhood offices of aldermen can sometimes help too.

ALL THAT GLITTERS . . .

Like the model apartment in a new building, the expensive color brochure you're handed as a prospective tenant glows. What it glows with are promises that will never be entirely fulfilled. The brochure was designed and printed about the time the building framework was topped off. As costs rose during construction, the lavish extras were slashed. It's up to you to ask which facilities actually exist—and what each costs to use.

The swimming pool isn't necessarily free. At Sandburg Village the outdoor pool is $65 per person per season, $110 for two people. Sandburg's tennis club costs $50, and the courts face the wrong way. At McClurg Court on Ontario St., use of sports facilities and health club runs $125-500. Its outdoor courts face east-west too.

It's up to you to ask. Is there a separate charge for air-conditioning? For heat? What will my electricity bill be? At Marina City, for instance, you pay for your heating unit and hot water unit. Charges for your use of both will appear on your electric bill. At Lake Point Towers in a big apartment, your electric bill can be $80 per month.

Ask what the lease demands you put down as floor covering. How much floor space must be covered with carpeting, how much may be tile? In some newer high rises, floors are unfinished; you buy carpeting from previous tenants or put down your own. One of the first concessions a new building makes when it's having trouble renting all its units is an offer of carpeting. Another is one to three months' free rent.

What are the other hidden costs—your TV hookup to the master antenna, parking in the garage, the laundry facilities, window washing, the Christmas tipping? If you're singles planning to share an apartment, how much more than the advertised rental will you have to pay? What will the charge be if one of your roommates leaves and management writes up a new lease to include a new roommate?

If you want to give up your apartment and sublet, what will that cost? Every building charges to draw up sublease forms, but that's rarely stated in your lease. Some buildings may not even allow subletting—check. Also ask if you'll be stuck with a second fixed amount for every month remaining on your lease to cover the cost of decorating for a new tenant. That's rarely, if ever, shown on a lease either. If you think you may be transferred before your lease expires, ask if the building has a 60-90 day provision called a transfer clause. What penalties are attached to it?

How much money do you have to deposit to have your *application* for a lease processed? (The application is a building's screening device, and the amount can be equal to a full month's rent. One knowledgeable real estate man says, "Tell 'em to go to hell," but others say a landlord would be crazy to rent, especially to young tenants, without one.) What happens to your money if you decide you don't want the apartment after all? If you do take the apartment, is the application fee applied to your first month's rent?

How much more will you have to pay for *execution* of the lease? Is this amount the so-called security deposit, or is it another separate fee?

If you rent in a building of more than 25 units and your security or rent deposit is more than $100 and management holds it more than six months, you're entitled to 4% annual interest. How—and when—will you get it? As cash or credit?

Rental agents are in business to rent apartments. They're not likely to point out building defects. Still, honorable agents will give honest answers—it's up to you to ask the right questions. In a high rise, for instance: "What happens in this building in high winds?" It never occurs to anyone that the Hancock with its particular cross-beam construction might creak. But when winds are high, it does, and in certain apartments the creaking is ferocious. In other high rises winds whistle in lobbies, corridors, apartments. The best time to decide about a particular high rise is on a foggy or stormswept day —not when a day is so clear you're carried away by a view.

LEASES

A Chicago lease on a heated, unfurnished apartment gives you exactly one right—the right to pay rent. If you accept a Chicago lease without question and sign it, you sign away all other rights.

Most new buildings create their own leases. Most older ones use Chicago Real Estate Board Form 12R. Its copyright is 1967, but it was conceived in 1936 and has scarcely changed since then. Almost all Chicago leases are rooted in medieval concepts of landlord-tenant relationships. For tenant, read serf. Apartment leases are considered nonnegotiable by landlords.

Regardless, you are going to try to negotiate some of the more abusive clauses in the lease. You will probably need a lawyer. Ask a friend if he can recommend one who handles leases for tenants. If you're a student, you can probably qualify for free legal help from a Legal Aid Bureau office. If you know no one, see "Not Clout but a Lawyer," p. 82.

HOW TO BEAT A LANDLORD

Before you sign an application for a lease, ask for a copy of the lease itself. The rental office in a high rise will probably refuse you. Be polite but insistent. Your argument is that you see no point in putting money down for a lease application—or having management go to the expense of processing it—unless you know what the lease will demand of you and that you'll be willing to sign it.

If you can't get a copy of the lease from the rental office, call the main office of the real estate firm that manages the building. Ask for a vice-president. Tell him what you want—and why. If he won't send you a copy of the lease, think twice about renting in that particular building and look elsewhere.

Get a copy of Chicago Real Estate Board Form 12R at Horder Stationers, 123 W. Washington or corner Lake & Wabash. Read every word; it's the basis of all Chicago leases, and you must understand it in order to protect yourself. Lessor is the landlord. Lessee is you.

The terms you want to negotiate in your lease are:

1. Security Deposits. These are standard—the equivalent of one month's rent. Tenants convinced they won't get their money back generally decide they won't pay the last month's rent—even though they know management will immediately threaten to sue. They figure that a note on their lawyer's letterhead will probably end the matter. If it doesn't they can plead their case in the Small Claims Municipal Division of Cook County Circuit Court at the Civic Center. They can do this without a lawyer. Or they ignore all and figure nobody's going to sue for one month's rent. Tenants afraid non-payment of the last month's rent will affect their ability to get another apartment pay up and write it off to experience.

2. Condition of Apartment, Upkeep. Make sure that whatever verbal agreement you reach on decorating is written into the lease. If it's not, you've signed a document that expressly states you examined the apartment, found it to your liking, were satisfied with its physical condition at the time you signed the lease.

Get attached to your lease a list of all visible defects in the apartment— cracks in plaster, mirrors, windows; cigarette burns or scratches on counter-tops; dirty oven, encrusted oven racks; chipped porcelain or tile; damaged fixtures, etc. This is how you protect your security deposit. You prove damages that existed before you moved in so you're not stuck for them when you move out.*

3. Fire & Casualty. Form 12R gives a landlord far too much latitude as to what he wants to do with your money and your apartment when a fire or

---

* If you plan to decorate with wallpaper, use only the kind with a backing that will steam off or vinyl paper that doesn't have a special backing. Management will charge at least $10 per hour if it has to steam off wallpaper, and it will not leave wallpaper up. The charges will be deducted from your security deposit. So will the cost of cleaning an apartment left in a grubby state, the cost of cleaning an encrusted oven, scouring a refrigerator, repairing a broken shower door (that you broke), and the like.

casualty for which you're not responsible makes your apartment uninhabitable. Large commercial tenants get options—why shouldn't you?

4. Confession of Judgment. This clause is vicious. Illinois is one of three states that allow it without limitation. Eighteen states have discontinued it as a matter of public policy. Confession of Judgment gives the landlord (lessor) the right to hire his lawyer or another lawyer to act for you (lessee). Your landlord's own lawyer acts for him. If two lawyers are involved, they trade off. If the landlord's lawyer represents you, he simply sticks in the name of another lawyer. Confession of Judgment is morally unconscionable because it translates as your landlord appointing a lawyer to act as your agent and accept a judgment against you. It's the same abuse that exists in Illinois credit contracts, and it's probably in every Chicago lease.

In some leases, say a Sandburg Village lease,* you won't find Confession of Judgment labeled as such. In the Sandburg lease it's buried at Clause **24**, Remedies, provision f:

> (f) Lessee hereby constitutes and irrevocably appoints any attorney of any court to be the true and lawful attorney of Lessee, and in name, place and stead of Lessee to appear for and on behalf of Lessee in any court of record at any time in any suit or suits brought against Lessee for the enforcement of any right hereunder by Lessor, to waive the issuance and service of process and trial by jury, from time to time, to confess judgment or judgments in favor of Lessor and against Lessee for any rent and interest thereon due hereunder by Lessee to Lessor and for costs of suit and for a reasonable attorney's fee in favor of Lessor to be fixed by the court, and to release all errors that may occur or intervene in such proceedings, including the issuance of execution upon any such judgment, and to stipulate that no appeal shall be prosecuted from such judgment or judgments, or that no proceedings in chancery or otherwise shall be filed or prosecuted to interfere in any way with the operation of such judgment or judgments or any execution issued thereon or with any supplemental proceedings taken by Lessor to collect the amount of any such judgment or judgments, and to consent that execution on any judgment or decree in favor of Lessor and against Lessee may issue forthwith.

Find this clause or its equivalent in the lease you're offered and get it out.

5. Waiver, or Waiver by Tenant. Waiver clauses mean you waive certain of your legal rights. Whenever you waive any of your rights, something is wrong. You'll probably need a lawyer's help to eliminate this clause, and you may not get an apartment if you insist on eliminating it, but you must try.

6. Strike any clause—it's usually under Abandonment or Remedies—that gives the landlord first lien on your things in your apartment (property in your premises) for any rent due. This clause is grossly improper.

7. Access. If your lease gives the landlord or his agent right of entry to your apartment for any reason other than to make repairs or to show the

---

* Arthur Rubloff owns.

apartment to prospective tenants during the last 90 days before the lease terminates, insist that this provision be changed. If you are a pretty young woman or two attractive young girls, this is essential for your own protection.

There are practical reasons for giving management a set of keys to your apartment—if you lock yourself out, how do you get in? If a pipe bursts or a fire breaks out, you'll want repairmen or firemen to get in.

8. Pets. Most buildings won't allow dogs. You might get the dog in if you suggest a rider to your lease stating you're 100% responsible for any damages by your dog. Also, produce his certificate proving he's been through obedience training.

9. Riders. Get in writing on a rider to your lease anything management promises—replacing tile, new refrigerator, whatever.

In leases for apartments in older buildings, especially on the Near North Side and in Lincoln Park, a landlord may insert a provision stating that if the building is sold or scheduled for demolition, you must vacate on 60-90 days' notice. This provision is usually inserted on a rider. If the building is a lovely old six-flat on Astor St., it means the owner knows that sooner or later a high-rise developer will come along with an offer to buy. The owner can make a better sale if he's not locked into two-year leases that have barely begun to expire. If it's a beautiful old building of 10 or 12 impressive apartments, the provision may also mean the owner is thinking of turning the building into a condominium.*

What do you do? You can refuse to sign. You may get away with it. More likely, the lessor won't rent to you. If you take the apartment on his terms, beware—and don't put any money into the place.

Keep Your Cool. You know what you're doing; you're not going to be bluffed. Management will tell you that not one of its tenants has asked for the terms you want, that you sign the lease as written or you don't get the apartment, that it will eliminate Confession of Judgment only if you pay double security deposit—this sort of thing. Politely insist management check with the downtown office. If the building has vacancies and you're a desirable tenant, you may win. If you don't, look elsewhere—there's not that much difference between buildings these days.

To Lease a House. The standard house lease has the same basic provisions as an apartment lease. Follow the procedure above. Ask for a net lease. It means you pay the taxes, but you also get the tax deduction. With a net lease, you'll be expected to handle repairs, but certain major repairs may still be the responsibility of landlord—for example, a wall collapses.

BUYING A CONDOMINIUM OR A HOUSE

Real estate taxes and operating costs have been skyrocketing in Chicago. If an owner can't turn a rental building into a condominium, taxes and operating costs are passed on to tenants as rent increases.† But because most

---

*Even if it's not a beautiful old building, it's likely the owner is considering turning it into a condominium.

† As much as 25% of your rent goes to pay real estate taxes.

apartment owners are thinking of conversion to condominiums, a tenant today is lucky if he can get a two-year lease—especially without an escalation clause for a 5-10% increase the second year. If you can afford to buy a condominium, buy it as a hedge against the next few years.

Whether you're buying a condominium or a house—

1. You're making the biggest investment of your life.

2. The sale to you is made by a broker, and because of the size of his commission, closing the sale is what the broker is most interested in doing.

3. You therefore do not trust any broker implicitly. You get a lawyer (p. 82). He may cost $300 or more, but it's the best money you'll ever spend. When you're spending $25,000 plus, $300 is lifetime insurance.

Do not sign anything—not even an Offer To Purchase (that's a contract) —until your lawyer has seen the papers. One reason: a new clause, allowed throughout Illinois, states that if, at the end of 60 days, you cannot close the contract, you forfeit the earnest money deposit ($1,000 or whatever) you'd put into escrow to make the purchase contract valid.

In the case of a house or of an older apartment building converted to a condominium, sign *nothing* until an architect has gone through the premises with you. He'll cost $150-200. Call the American Institute of Architects for a referral, 842-4634. Or get a contractor capable of checking structural soundness, plumbing, electric lines, etc. Problems will lie in inadequate wiring, old plumbing, old heating units, hidden steel beams that make remodeling a nightmare.*

The city has an ordinance prohibiting display of "For Sale" signs on houses (to prevent blockbusting). To learn about available houses, check classified ads or work with a real estate firm that subscribes to a multiple listing service. Most, if not all, brokers dealing in houses (p. 29) do.

Or clue into a neighborhood that appeals to you through its local community organization (other than its local chamber of commerce). For instance: Lincoln Park Conservation Assn. (LPCA), 2373 N. Lincoln, 477-5100, knows what's available in old private homes and new town-house construction and will also refer you to local sources for mortgage money. Pullman Civic Organization, 644 E. 113th, 785-5557, has a real estate division that matches you with housing opportunities at no charge.

Or find a well-regarded neighborhood real estate broker and work with him. Figure he's got to maintain his reputation in the neighborhood because that's where his business is. He may not be any more trustworthy than any other broker, but he's less likely to shaft you—simply because if he does, you'll badmouth him.

Financing. Buying a home is just like buying a car. You don't let the car salesman arrange financing for you—you go to your bank and make your own arrangements. Similarly, you don't let a real estate broker arrange your mortgage. Do it yourself; shop for a mortgage to see what the market is.

(The one possible exception to the above is if you're buying into a development where the developer has made very favorable arrangements with a particular savings and loan association.)

---

* So will Chicago's permits to build or remodel. Ask neighbors how they handle these.

Start with the local S/L in the suburb or city neighborhood where you're planning to buy. Check S/Ls in town* and your bank and another full-service bank. The maximum a bank in Metropolitan Chicago generally loans is 75% for up to 25 years. The maximum an S/L generally loans is 90% for 30 years. The amount of the mortgage is going to reflect your income, number of dependents, and the location of the house you want to buy.

Any bank or S/L will send an appraiser to look at the property; the appraisal will give you an idea of the fairness of a real estate broker or developer's asking price; it will also reflect the location of the house.

Home Investments Fund, 116 S. Michigan, 641-1035, offers members of racial minorities advice and assistance on financing. The organization is nonprofit, specializes in fair housing services.

---

* First Federal, Talman, and Bell are the biggest S/Ls in town, followed by Home Federal and Chicago Federal.

CHAPTER II

NOT GETTING LOST

How Streets Are Numbered. This is one sprawling city, but it tries to be scientific about its street numbering system. Almost every block is numbered successively by 100. The numbering system begins in the Loop at the intersection of State and Madison streets, which have been arbitrarily designated as zero. Example: the block from Madison north to Washington contains numbers between 1 and 100, and the next block north from Washington to Randolph contains numbers from 101 to 200.

Here's how the system works. Say you're going to the Illinois Dept. of Motor Vehicles Office at 5301 W. Lexington for a driver's license. The address tells you the location is 53 blocks west of State—but where is Lexington? You either have to ask or else look it up in a street guide (find one in the front of *Yellow Pages B*). The answer is 732 south, which means seven blocks south of Madison. Any complete city street map will show you the fastest way to get there. See p. 44 for the best maps and how to get them.

Why It's Easy To Get Lost. The street numbering system fails where Chicago's grid system fails. The grid is shot through with diagonal streets that jog and angle. On diagonal streets like Archer, Ogden, and Fifth, the street numbering patterns are at wild variance to the system that routinely numbers diagonal streets on a north-south basis. Ogden and Fifth are numbered on an east-west basis. But Ogden is also numbered north-south as it jogs along like the old Indian trail it once was. Archer's numbering system makes no sense whatsoever until it reaches Narragansett and heads west.

On the North and Northwest Sides of the city, especially, streets angle off major diagonals, come together at five- and six-way intersections, cross railroad tracks at grade, are blocked by cemeteries and may or may not pick up on the other side. Streets that look like they'll cross the North Branch of the Chicago River dead-end in industrial sites or make 90° turns under viaducts or are interrupted by expressways. Smart motorists do not set out for unfamiliar parts of the city without plotting their course with a street guide and map. A street guide's essential because street name signs aren't adequate.

Street Name Signs. Fully half the street name signs have been installed by dolts who mounted them on the left sides of intersections that you, the driver, are approaching. The only way to read those signs is to look back once you're half-across the intersection; not easy.

The other problem with street name signs is that almost none of them give enough information. They give a single designation—either the street name or number. ("Delaware," say, or "55th St." but never the convenience of "Delaware—900 North.") New Yorkers, accustomed to an unhelpful numbering system, automatically give directions in terms of intersecting streets—Fifth and 73rd. Chicagoans, lulled by the false security of a system that counts off *all* streets from one fixed starting point, don't. But an address like 666 W. Wrightwood is almost meaningless unless you know where Wrightwood is. Get in the habit of asking "Wrightwood and what?" Then ask if Wrightwood is north or south and numerically how far north or south.

Using Numbers on Light Poles. New green- or gray-painted light poles on most major streets are marked at pedestrian eye level with vertical numbers— for instance, $\frac{29}{3}$.* The top number tells you approximately what hundred block you're in. Read as 29 blocks from State & Madison. Don't try to read numbers on expressway light poles—they refer only to Commonwealth Edison circuits.

Chicago's Principal Streets and Their Distances from State & Madison

(East-west streets parallel Madison; north-south parallel State)

NORTH FROM MADISON STREET

Miles	House Nos.	Street Names	Miles	House Nos.	Street Names
4/5	600	Ohio St.	6	4800	Lawrence Av.
1	800	Chicago Av.	6½	5200	Foster Av.
1½	1200	Division St.	7	5600	Bryn Mawr Av.
2	1600	North Av.	7½	6000	Peterson Av.
2½	2000	Armitage Av.	8	6400	Devon Av.
3	2400	Fullerton Av.	8½	6800	Pratt Av.
3½	2800	Diversey Av.	9	7200	Touhy Av.
4	3200	Belmont Av.	9½	7600	Howard St.
4½	3600	Addison St.	9¾	7800	Juneway Terrace
5	4000	Irving Park Rd.			(South line of Calvary Cemetery
5½	4400	Montrose Av.			forms city limits farthest north)

SOUTH FROM MADISON STREET

Miles	House Nos.	Street Names	Miles	House Nos.	Street Names
½	600	Harrison St.	9	7900	79th St.
1	1200	Roosevelt Rd.	9½	8300	83rd St.
1½	1600	16th St.	10	8700	87th St.
2	2200	Cermak Rd.	10½	9100	91st St.
2½	2600	26th St.	11	9500	95th St.
3	3100	31st St.	11½	9900	99th St.
3½	3500	35th St.	12	10300	103rd St.
4	3900	Pershing Rd.	12½	10700	107th St.
4½	4300	43rd St.	13	11100	111th St.
5	4700	47th St.	13½	11500	115th St.
5½	5100	51st St.	14	11900	119th St.
6	5500	55th St.	14½	12300	123rd St.
6½	5900	59th St.	15	12700	127th St.
7	6300	63rd St.	15½	13100	131st St.
7½	6700	67th St. (Marquette Rd.)	16	13500	135th St.
8	7100	71st St.	16⅜	13800	138th St.
8½	7500	75th St.			(City limits farthest south)

WEST FROM STATE STREET

Miles	House Nos.	Street Names	Miles	House Nos.	Street Names
1	800	Halsted St.	5½	4400	Kostner Av.
1½	1200	Racine Av.	6	4800	Cicero Av.
2	1600	Ashland Av.	6½	5200	Laramie Av.
2½	2000	Damen Av.	7	5600	Central Av.
3	2400	Western Av.	7½	6000	Austin Av.
3½	2800	California Av.	8	6400	Narragansett Av.
4	3200	Kedzie Av.	8½	6800	Oak Park Av.
4½	3600	Central Park Av.	9	7200	Harlem Av.
5	4000	Pulaski Rd. (Crawford Av.)			

EAST FROM STATE STREET

(At State and Madison Sts., the lakefront is ⅝ mile east)

Miles	House Nos.	Street Names	Miles	House Nos.	Street Names
½	400	King Dr.	3½	2800	Manistee Av.
1	800	Cottage Grove Av.	4	3200	Brandon Av.
1½	1200	Woodlawn Av.	4½	3600	Avenue L
2	1600	Stony Island Av.	5⅛	4100	State Line Rd.
2½	2000	Jeffery Blvd.			(City limits farthest east)
3	2400	Yates Blvd.			

* Bottom number is useful only for reporting dead light.

Expressways, Tollways, Major Routes. Chicagoans use names rather than route numbers when they give expressway or tollway directions. Free maps that you get at gas stations are only beginning to show both. These are the major routes (I = Interstate):

Adlai E. Stevenson Expy = I-55 = the Southwest Expy
Cermak Rd. = 22nd St.
Dan Ryan Expy = I-90 and I-94; splits into Calumet Expy (I-94) and I-57 at about 99th St.
Dwight D. Eisenhower Expy = I-90
East-West Tollway = Ill. 190
Edens Expy = I-94
Harlem Av. = Ill. 43; becomes Waukegan Rd. in suburbs
Higgins Rd. = Ill. 72
John F. Kennedy Expy = I-94, also Ill. 194
King Dr. = Doctor Martin Luther King, Jr. Dr.
Lake Cook Rd. = County Line Rd. west of Edens Expy
Lake Shore Dr. = the Outer Drive = the Drive = US 41
Lincoln Hwy = US 30
North Av. = Ill. 64
Northwest Hwy = US 14
Northwest Tollway = I-90 and Ill. 194
Ogden Av. = US 34, also US 66
Rand Rd. = US 12
Roosevelt Rd. = 12th St. in town, Ill. 38 west of town
Skyway = Chicago Skyway (tollway) = I-90
Tri-State Tollway = I-294 and I-94

Rush Hour Traffic Broadcasts. Radio station WGN (720 on AM dial) broadcasts instant traffic information on tollways, expressways, and major Chicago thoroughfares at 15- to 20-minute intervals from 6:55 AM to 9:05 AM and 4:15 PM to 6:32 PM, Mon.-Fri. Also from Memorial Day through Labor Day, Sunday night reentry weekend traffic from 6:05 PM to 9:30 PM.

Hazarding the Loop. During business hours the Loop is a mess: 173,000 cars daily. Trucks make every kind of delivery in daytime hours; illegal parking negates the usefulness of one-way streets;* drivers snake around El-track pillars and cars line up to get in or out of parking facilities. State St. is full of restrictions as to where you can or can't turn. Foul weather creates a traffic drag of 4 mph. Parking charges are exorbitant except at the fringes of the Loop (p. 51). Abandon your car for bus, subway, commuter train, or cab.

Short-Cutting the Loop. Lower Wacker Dr., generally called the lower level or the underground, is a fast way around the Loop from 500 north to 500 south. It runs under Michigan Av. from Grand Av., across the lower level of the Michigan Av. Bridge, then under Wacker to the starting point of the Eisenhower Expy and the interchanges into Dan Ryan and Kennedy Expys. You can enter at Grand, one block east of Rush. It's a two-way drive—the only traffic is car and truck—and you can move along at a nice clip even during rush

---

*All east-west streets in the Loop from Lake to Van Buren are one-way streets alternating direction every block; Lake is eastbound, Randolph westbound, Washington eastbound, etc. Dearborn is one-way northbound, Clark one-way southbound.

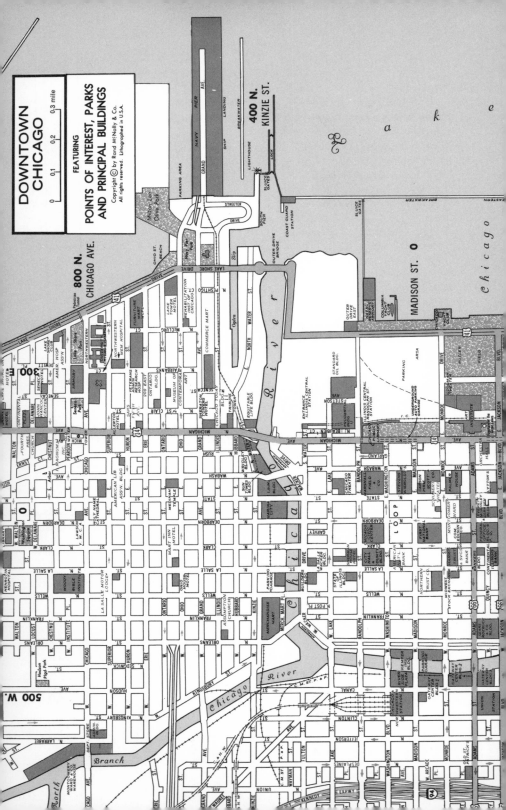

DOWNTOWN CHICAGO

FEATURING
POINTS OF INTEREST, PARKS AND PRINCIPAL BUILDINGS

0   0.1   0.2   0.3 mile

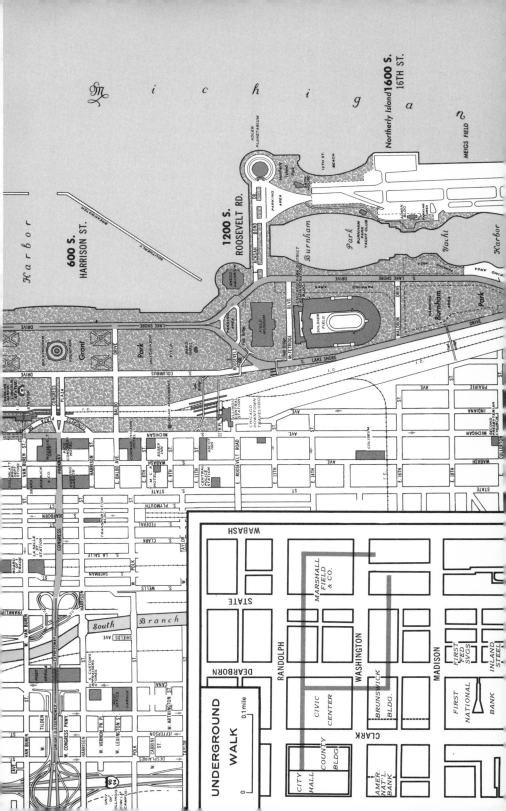

hours. The Eisenhower heading east is the only expressway from which you can enter the underground.* Other entries and exits to lower Wacker: Kinzie St., Illinois St., Garland Ct., Garvey Ct., Post Pl., Randolph St., and Monroe St. Find these the same way everyone else does—through trial and error or by phoning the city's Dept. of Public Works (Bureau of Engineering), 744-3618.

Pedestrian Undergrounds. You *can* walk lower Wacker, and hundreds of people use it in bad weather to cross under the Michigan Av. Bridge. Except on the lower bridge, be prepared for athletics because there are no formal sidewalks—only catwalks that edge buildings between high loading docks—which means you're jumping up and down all the way.

Under Washington from Wabash to LaSalle. You can walk underground from Marshall Field & Co. to the Civic Center-County Bldg.-City Hall. Entrance is through Field's Budget Floor at CTA subway sign just beyond the cafeteria. Head for the subway, pass the ticket office, follow signs "To Dearborn Street." Go past the Dearborn subway station to the lower concourse of the Civic Center. Signs point the way to County Bldg.-City Hall a block west and to the Brunswick Bldg. a block south on Washington between Dearborn and Clark. The concourse is a shopping center of sorts. See map p. 41.

Public Transportation. Lacking a car, you get around Chicago by CTA (Chicago Transit Authority) buses or rapid transit system of subways and elevated trains. CTA operates 134 different bus lines and 9 rapid transit lines. None are bargains except the no-transfer-needed Howard St. El to 63rd and the Lake St. El from Harlem to the Loop and into the Dan Ryan to 95th. Free CTA maps (p. 44) are helpful, and so is CTA 24-hour information service when you can get on the line—during business hours it can be impossible. Phone 664-7220 or 664-7200.

At night, buses are safer than subways and Els, simply because they're at ground level and visible and everyone's in the same cabin with the driver. Still, subways and Els are safe enough if you're not alone or two young women alone. If you're a student or secretary, start thinking in terms of small groups—two girls and a guy, two couples, three and two, whatever.

Fares. You must have exact fare on buses—drivers can't make change. Transfers 10¢.

Adults: 45¢; across-Loop shuttle bus from Soldier Field Parking Lot to Merchandise Mart 35¢.

Children: Under age 7 free when accompanied by adult; ages 7-11 with CTA ID card 20¢.

Senior Citizens: 20¢ with free CTA ID card.

Taxicabs. Chicago cabs are expensive, and the owners of all cab companies have ceased caring whether the cabs are clean, comfortable, and in good repair. Just pulling away from a curb costs 40¢, and meters jump by 10¢ every

---

* Entrance is via a ramp off the right-hand lane of the Eisenhower just past the main post office. The ramp, marked "Wacker Drive," curves and dips under the Eisenhower, surfaces briefly, then gives you a choice of upper or lower Wacker.

2/7 of a mile (shown on meter in ¼ mile units). The first mile averages 70¢; all other miles average 35¢ each. Additional riders are charged 20¢ each if over age 12. Despite this wholly unnecessary charge and all other drawbacks, cabs are still the best transportation to the Near North Side, Old Town, Mid North, and the Loop, where parking is either nonexistent or overpriced.

You're lucky if a college student with long hair is your driver. He won't drive like a maniac, won't grump about the problems of being a cabby, won't refuse to lower the level of the cab's irritating intercom, and is almost always polite.

In this city you can phone for a cab:

Yellow Cab, CA 5-6000   Checker Cab, MO 6-3700

Flash Cab, LO 1-1444   American United, BI 8-7600

Some examples of fares: O'Hare Airport to Palmer House (20 miles) $10; Field's to Museum of Science & Industry $4-5; Field's to Old Town, say North Av. & Wells, $1.75-2.25. Suburbs immediately adjacent to Chicago are included in metered fares. Beyond these, the driver must phone his company for permission to take you deeper into suburbia and also to get the flat rate (Checker, for instance, $10.50 from Loop to Winnetka). No cabby may refuse to accept a passenger unless his "Not for Hire" sign is showing. No cabby can refuse to take you to any city address you give. (If he does refuse, tell him to first take you to the nearest police station.) In bad neighborhoods, cab companies may refuse to make a phoned-in pickup; ask where the nearest cabstand is, and take public transportation to it.

Jitney cabs operate illegally along bus lines in black neighborhoods. Fare 25¢ per person in a cab that may be shared by as many as five people. Major South Side route these days is along King Dr. from 29th to 63rd.

Airport Limousine Service. Continental Air Transport, 726-8720

To O'Hare Airport: 24-hour service from Palmer House, Pick-Congress, Hilton, and Sheraton-Chicago approximately every 15 minutes during peak travel hours. From Executive House, 7 AM-8 PM every half hour. From Holiday Inn (Lake Shore Dr.), Water Tower Hyatt House, Continental Plaza, Drake, Playboy Towers, Ambassadors East and West, at half-hour intervals. Check—schedules change. Fare $2.60.

To Midway Airport: Service from Palmer House, Hilton, Pick-Congress only, every half hour 6 AM-7:30 PM. Schedules change on weekends, holidays—phone. Fare $2.25.

Helicopter Service to O'Hare & Midway Airports. Chicago Helicopter Airways, 767-2380. Five round trips daily to each airport from Meigs Field, plus Midway-O'Hare flights. Fare one way $10.80. Reserve at least one day in advance.

Loop Commuter Train Stations (and lines they serve)

Chicago & North Western Station, 500 W. Madison, 332-2121
Chicago & North Western
LaSalle St. Station, 139 W. Van Buren, WA 2-3200
Rock Island Lines
Randolph St. Station, 151 N. Michigan, 332-0295
Chicago, South Shore & South Bend Electric; Illinois Central Gulf

Union Station, Canal & Adams, 346-5200
Burlington Northern; Illinois Central Gulf; Milwaukee Road; Penn Central; Santa Fe

Loop Commuter Bus Service
Chicago Greyhound Terminal, Clark & Randolph, 346-5000
Greyhound; Indian Trails; Indiana Motor Bus; West Suburban Transit
Other Suburban Bus Lines
South Suburban Safeway, 468-0051
Suburban Transit System, HI 5-3831
United Motor Coach, 824-2111
Valley Transit, 458-5150
West Towns Bus, AU 7-3842

Note: CTA provides connecting service to some suburban lines, also some direct service to suburbs. Call 664-7220 or 664-7200.

Intercity Trains. All Amtrak trains arrive and depart Union Station, Canal & Adams, 786-1333. Ticket office also at Jackson & Michigan. **Rock Island** intercity uses LaSalle St. Station (see preceding page).

Bicycle "Safety" Routes. Literally thousands of Chicagoans are bike commuters into the Loop, but the city has scarcely begun to concern itself with cyclist needs. So-called bicycle commuter safety routes (as distinguished from the lakefront bike path) have been designated in the Lincoln Park area, on the Near North Side, and in Hyde Park with white-on-green signs that say "Bike Route." The routes are located mainly along collector and local streets but only two streets have separate bicycling lanes and then only during rush hour: Clark, southbound between Elm and Wacker, 7-9:30 AM; Dearborn, northbound between Wacker and Oak, 4-6 PM. *Cyclist's Rights & Responsibilities* maps all routes and includes bicycle traffic regulations. Get it and registration information from Commissioner of Streets & Sanitation, Room 700, City Hall, 744-8020. Registration free, mandatory.

Useful Maps and Guides. Standard Oil's free map of the city and suburbs is super. Its color demarcations are good, every street is beautifully marked. The map shows high schools, hospitals, public golf courses, parks, museums, commuter train stations, individual buildings in the Loop and at the University of Chicago, individual airline terminals and runways at O'Hare, oases on the tollways and toll plazas.

CTA maps of bus routes, rapid transit routes, and all lines combined, free in rapid transit stations or CTA Public Information Dept., P.O. Box 3555, Chicago 60654.

New Chicago Street Guide (Rand McNally). A complete city street guide with map, $1.

Official Illinois Highway Map. Free from state of Illinois, Dept. of Public Works & Buildings, 300 N. State, 793-2284.

Illinois Tollway Map. Shows all entries and exits to tollways and expressways. Free at any manned tollbooth or call 654-2200.

CHAPTER III

INSTANT CITY

INSTANT ACTION

Fire, FI 7-1313

Police Emergency, PO 5-1313

Cook County Sheriff's Police Emergency, GL 8-1000

Du Page County Sheriff's Police Emergency, 668-0900

Kane County Sheriff's Police Emergency, 232-8400

Lake County Sheriff's Police Emergency, 623-1855

McHenry County Sheriff's Police Emergency, 815-338-2141

Will County Sheriff's Police Emergency, 815-727-6191

State Highway Police. For Cook County north of Roosevelt Rd., AV 3-2400; south of Roosevelt Rd., 385-2121

Coast Guard Rescue, 768-8000

LIVE & RECORDED INFORMATION

For Chicago Police Dept. Information, 744-4000

    Missing Person, 744-6222

    For individual police districts, see Police Dept. under "Chicago—City of" in *Chicago A.*

Correct Local Time, CA 8-8000

Sports Scores, *Sun-Times,* WH 3-3080; *Daily News,* CE 6-2200; *Tribune & Chicago Today,* 222-1234

Stock Market Reports (Dial-A-Stock), WE 9-1600

WEATHER

Chicago & Vicinity Weather, WE 4-1212. Taped message from National Weather Service for city and counties within 75 miles of Chicago. Temperatures given hourly. Forecasts written at 4:15 AM, 10 AM, 4:15 PM, 10 PM. Forecast at 10 AM covers weather for current day, evening, following day; 10 PM forecast covers weather for next day and second day after. Forecasts aren't nearly as accurate as could be wished, though NWS claims 88% accuracy on temperatures and precipitation. As alternatives, catch Channel 5's meteorologist, Harry Volkman (he does his own forecast), during the 5 PM and 10 PM newscasts or WIND's meteorologist, Earl Finckle, at 6:30 AM, 7:30 AM, 8:30 AM, 4:30 PM, and 5:30 PM.

Midwest Extended Outlook, 922-3251. An entirely different NWS recording that includes Lake Michigan wave and weather conditions for recreational sailing in summer; road conditions in winter; three-day forecast year-round for Illinois, Indiana, Michigan, Wisconsin, and thus as early as any Wednesday, a forecast for the weekend.

Weekend Weather. Year-round from Channel 7's meteorologist, John Coleman, Fridays at 7:30 AM, 8 AM, 5 PM, 6 PM, and 10 PM.

Nationwide Forecast, 247-4612. Next-day weather across the country and in selected cities. Also from NWS.

Pilot Weather Briefing at O'Hare Airport, 686-2156

Midwest Road Conditions, 827-7101. Taped messages from Nov. to April for Illinois and surrounding states. If no message, assume roads are clear. For northern Cook County, phone State Police in Elgin, 742-3553; for southern Cook County, State Police in Blue Island, 385-2121. For tollway conditions, Illinois State Toll Highway Authority, 654-2200.

Ski Weather Reports (in season), CE 6-SNOW

ILLINOIS BELL TELEPHONE SERVICES

Telephone Information Assistance, 411

Phone Out-of-Order, 611

Long Distance Operator, 211

Long Distance Information. To get the telephone number and address of any person or business anywhere in the country, dial his (its) Area Code plus 555-1212. The operator who answers will provide the information. Find Area Codes for large cities in *Chicago A* or dial Operator or call the Social Sciences Dept. at Chicago Public Library, CE 6-8922. This department also has some overseas addresses and phone numbers and the *International Yellow Pages*.

Telephone Name & Address Service, 796-9600. When a private switchboard operator or private answering service merely gives you a phone number to call, this helpful Bell Telephone service furnishes the missing name and address for any Chicago number.

Note: Illinois Bell charges 30¢ if you dial an operator to place a local call that you can dial yourself. The 30¢ charge covers the first three minutes of your call; you're then charged 10¢ for each additional minute. These charges appear on your bill. Operators should waive them if you cannot reach a called number after repeated attempts to place a call—but you must tell operator you're up against transmission problems and you must ask for waived charges.

A blind or handicapped person who must have operator help to make calls is not charged if he identifies himself as blind or handicapped.

FOR DRIVERS & CAR OWNERS

The state of Illinois is concerned with your driver's license, license plates, title and registration of your car. The city of Chicago and some suburbs insist on a yearly tax stamp, which must be on your windshield.

Newcomers must prove car ownership. Lacking a title, phone Dept. of Motor Vehicles office, ES 9-5600, for instructions.

Driver's License. All newcomers must get an Illinois driver's license within 90 days after establishing permanent residency. Fee $8. Go to Dept. of Motor Vehicles facilities for application and tests. Tests are three-part: eye exam, written exam, and driving.* Hours 8 AM-10 PM, Mon.-Fri. Offices located at:

In city	In suburbs
5301 W. Lexington, ES 9-5600	Lombard, 837 S. Westmore, 629-0380
5401 N. Elston, 282-4000	Waukegan, 2712 Grand, 662-7171
9901 S. King Dr., CO 4-5700	Elgin, 419 Dundee, 741-5785
	Joliet, 2018 Jefferson, 815-725-5262

These facilities also handle for all residents: auto title transfer; application for license plates; transfer of license plates; application for change of address or other correction on driver's license; replacement of lost license; new resident's motor vehicle use tax clearance.

Secretary of State Walk-in Facility, 150 W. Randolph, 793-5540. Handles all of above except driving test and motor vehicle use tax clearance. Hours 9 AM-5:30 PM, Mon.-Fri.

Note: Before taking driver's test, read *Illinois Rules of the Road*. It's fairly specific, and the written and driver's tests are based on it. Free at any Dept. of Motor Vehicles facility or any currency exchange that sells license plates. Also available in Spanish, Italian, Polish, German.

License Plates. Buy them over the counter at the above driver's license facilities, or mail applications to Secretary of State, Springfield, 62756 (plates should arrive in about 21 days). Or purchase at various banks between Dec. 1 and Feb. 15. Service fee $1. In the Loop: First National, One First National Plaza; Continental Illinois, 231 S. LaSalle; Mercantile National, 222 S. Riverside Plaza. Some neighborhood and suburban banks offer the same service—ask around.

Vehicle Sticker (Tax Stamp). In Chicago, City Clerk's office (see below); in suburbs, City or Village Hall. Show title or bill of sale. After initial purchase of sticker, Chicago sends computer printout at renewal time. Fill in blanks, attach check or money order, get sticker by mail.

Note: Currency exchanges will get license plates for you, handle applications for transfer of title, and provide vehicle sticker. Service fees vary from one currency exchange to another but are generally $2-2.50 per service.

CHICAGO'S GOVERNMENT

City Hall, 121 N. LaSalle, 744-4000. City Hall is both the building on LaSalle and the government of Chicago. You can live here for years without ever going into City Hall because items like dog licenses can be handled by phone inquiry and a check sent by mail.

City Clerk's Office, Room 107, performs numerous functions including:
City Vehicle Sticker, 744-6878
Dog License, 744-6875
Gun Registration, 744-8100
Hunting & Fishing Licenses, 744-6882
Complaints Against the City (forms for). See p. 87.

---

* A racket exists in connection with the driving test. See "Fixes & Bribes," p. 90.

City Council, 744-6800. More Chicagoans ought to see City Council in action, for it's a unique presentation of the way the city is run. As one citizen says, "You can see the arrogance of power in action." Also fascinating: the explosions when the handful of independent aldermen take a stand and have to be answered. Every other Wednesday beginning leisurely after 10 AM.

Aldermen's Offices. Located in City Hall. For aldermanic information, 744-3081.

Board of Election Commissioners,* DE 2-3050. Register here to vote—or wait for precinct registration. Get absentee ballots here.

Mayor's Office of Inquiry & Information, 744-3370. For questions about city functions and some complaints such as lack of heat and garbage pickup. See also p. 86.

Municipal Reference Library, 744-4992. Will answer specific, *single* question about the city, especially statistical. Short answer only.

Board of Health, Civic Center, 744-4000; health inquiries, 744-4340. Contact about health hazards such as flooded home, nonworking drain landlord won't fix, rat-infested garbage, vermin, and dirty public facilities—e.g., restaurants, washrooms. Sometimes it may help you.

Board of Education, 228 N. LaSalle, 641-4141

Commission on Human Relations, 640 N. LaSalle, 744-4111 (24-hour phone). Administers the city's civil rights laws through divisions that handle fair housing, equal employment opportunity, public accommodation. This last deals with problems rising from discrimination due to sex, nationality, religion, or race in restaurants, schools, hospitals, etc.

Dept. of Human Resources, 640 N. LaSalle, 744-4045. Concerns itself with child-youth needs and needs of senior citizens.

Traffic Ticket Information & Traffic Court, 321 N. LaSalle, 321-6080

Environmental Control, 320 N. Clark, 744-4080

Chicago Park District, 294-2200. Not governed by City Hall but a city facility nevertheless. Call for information about scheduled activities; recreational facilities; special programs for handicapped or mentally retarded children and adults; arts, crafts, drama, and other lessons at field houses. Mon.-Fri. Also weekends between Memorial Day and Labor Day.

Note: To complain about inadequate city services or request needed city services, see p. 86.

COOK COUNTY GOVERNMENT

County Bldg., 118 N. Clark, 443-5500. Different address, same building as City Hall. Come here for:

Marriage License, 443-5663

Marriage Court, 443-5660

County Clerk, Election Registration, 443-5666. If you live in an unincor-

---

* The board conducts and supervises elections for Chicago, Cicero, Berwyn, Stickney, and Lyons.

porated town with no election registration facilities, this office can tell you where to register and vote.

Taxpayer Assistance, 443-8920. For help with any questions about basis of tax assessment of your property and ways to appeal.

Recorder of Deeds & Registrar of Torrens Titles, 443-5500. Record deeds of personal real estate here, locate prior real estate transactions, find out what you're in for if you're faced with a lien on your property or a judgment.

Birth Certificates, Bureau of Vital Statistics, 130 N. Wells, 443-7790

Public Aid, 318 W. Adams, 368-1551

Cook County Forest Preserves, CO 1-8400. Call for information about recreational facilities, snow or ice conditions for skiing or pond skating, nature centers, berry and nut picking, Palos Park Farm, maps of various preserves, collection centers for recycling of waste products. Mon.-Fri., but occasionally on weekends a ranger on duty can be helpful.

STATE SERVICES

State of Illinois Bldg., 160 N. LaSalle, 793-3500. Come here for:
  Governor's Office, 793-2121
  State Income Tax Information, 641-2150. From suburbs, ask operator if the toll-free number is in service.

State Unemployment Compensation, 165 N. Canal, 793-4000
  Benefit Claims Information, 793-4195

Public Aid Dept., 209 W. Jackson, 793-2626

Note: For complaints to **Illinois Fair Employment Practices Commission, Illinois Commerce Commission,** other state offices, see "Clout & Savvy."

FEDERAL SERVICES

Everett McKinley Dirksen Bldg., 219 S. Dearborn, 353-4242
  Passports, 353-5426 (recorded 24-hour message); 353-7155 (live information during business hours)
  IRS Taxpayer Information, 641-1040
  Economic Stabilization Dept. (enforcement arm of Cost of Living Council), 591-1229
  Immigration & Naturalization, 353-7334
  Social Security Administration, 239-7000
  Civil Service Commission, 353-5136
  FBI, 431-1333. Only handles cases involving bank robbery, extortion, kidnapping, fraud against the federal government, assault on federal officer, bomb threats, interstate auto theft, hijacking of planes, espionage.

Medicare, 233 N. Michigan, 239-7000. For eight other city locations, plus suburbs, see "Medicare" in *Chicago A.*

Veterans Administration, 2030 W. Taylor, 353-3900

Peace Corps, One N. Wacker, 353-4990

Small Business Administration, 219 S. Dearborn, 353-4528

Post Office (main bldg.), 433 W. Van Buren, 353-2420. If general information line above is busy, use:
1st class, 353-2421
4th class, 353-2671
Foreign, 353-2677
Sunday, after 5 PM, holidays, 353-2420

AIRPORTS

Chicago-O'Hare International Airport, bounded by Mannheim, Touhy, Irving Park, and York, 686-2200. The world's busiest airport—generally a madhouse because of snarled traffic and swarms of travelers.

At rush hours, the fastest way to O'Hare is often via CTA O'Hare express bus #40. The bus goes nonstop from Jefferson Park Rapid Transit Terminal, 4917 N. Milwaukee (near Lawrence). Fare 75¢. Any northbound Congress-Milwaukee or Douglas-Milwaukee rapid transit train speeds right to Jefferson Park Terminal—pay 55¢ boarding the El; it includes transfer so you pay an additional 20¢ for the O'Hare bus. Buses leave on the half hour 4 AM to midnight, then hourly. Starting from the Loop, total travel time can be as fast as 45 minutes.

Students from the University of Chicago make the entire trip from the South Side to O'Hare for 75¢ by starting on the South Side El and transferring.

When You Might Miss Your Plane. Avoid traffic congestion on the Departures ramp by using the lower-level Arrivals ramp. Hop out at your terminal, escalate up.

Luggage Carts. O'Hare owns 500 luggage carts, and they're supposed to be at strategic places in all terminals. They aren't. The sky caps hide them behind lockers near escalators, behind phone booths, in or behind baggage departments, behind Lost & Found departments, under staircases, and in any other obscure, dark area that exists. The sky caps, after all, are Chicagoans, and they're just doing business Chicago-style. When desperate, ask where the wheelchairs are kept and don't let a sky cap get it for you—go for it yourself; a few luggage carts will always be stacked alongside.

Parking. Lot parking costs 65¢ for 4 hours or less, $3.15 per 24 hours. The parking structure ingests 9,500 cars at same rates. Shuttle bus service to terminals is good.

Departing O'Hare by cab is an unpleasant example of 1970s dehumanization. O'Hare has just two cab starters. You're expected to lug your suitcases to one of them and queue. The starter may be a couple of blocks away, but no matter—you go to him because he's got a stranglehold on the cabs. If the waiting group is 190 or more deep, take the escalator in the nearest terminal up to Departures. When a cab pulls up and a departee gets out, leap innocently in. O'Hare cab starters frown on this expediency but can't stop it. You're not breaking any law—only a starter's notion of his own rule.

Midway Airport, 5700 S. Cicero, PO 7-0500. Not as busy as O'Hare and probably never will be pushed to its capacity as O'Hare is. All major airlines but

Continental and Braniff use Midway, fly mainly to New York, Washington, D.C., Twin Cities.

Meigs Field, 1500 south, on a peninsula in the lake, 744-4787. Use for helicopter service to O'Hare and Midway; for shuttle flights to towns like Detroit, Madison, Fort Wayne; and for private planes. If a shuttle flight goes to your destination, take it rather than a jet. It will closely match a jet's arrival time and will land at an airport closer in.

Note: For airport limousine and helicopter service, see p. 43.

PARKING

In the Loop. All-day parking in the Loop sets you back a minimum of $3.25 in private facilities. The only bargain parking handy to the Loop is in fringe areas, behind the Merchandise Mart ($1.25-2 all day), in lots on Grand Av. like the Ganser-Oguss lot at 351 E. Grand ($1.90, 5-24 hrs.), in Marina Parking, and in the city-owned Grant Park complex of Monroe St. lot ($1.50, 16 hrs.). Self-parking in the two city-owned undergrounds in Grant Park, $3 for 9 hours. Special night rate starting at 5 PM, $1.25, can be prepaid.

Grant Park south underground garage runs from Congress to Adams, is never as crowded as the north underground garage (Randolph to Monroe), and has the greater capacity—three parking levels. Ramp entrance at Michigan & Van Buren (for northbound traffic).

Find ramp entrance to Grant Park north underground garage at Randolph & Michigan (for southbound traffic). You can't drive underground from one garage to the other, probably because the city couldn't burrow under the Art Institute.

Self-parking for both underground garages, first hour $1; each additional hour to 6 hours 25¢; 6-12 hours $2.50.

The city owns about 65 parking facilities. Five are in the Loop. Rates vary but are generally one hour 65-75¢; two hours 85-90¢; each additional hour 25¢. For free map of all locations, write Dept. of Streets & Sanitation, Bureau of Parking, 54 W. Hubbard. Rates aren't included, but you can get them by phoning 744-4501.

On the Near North Side. No better than in the Loop. If you're going to shop or lunch on North Michigan Av. or see physicians in the area and every parking facility is full, park in small lots on Clark and cab over.

The most expensive parking lot on the Near North Side is at the corner of Oak & Michigan (1 hr. or less $1.90; 2 hrs. or less $2.65; 3 hrs. or less $3.40). The most expensive garage is in the John Hancock—it's also the slowest to retrieve your car (up to 40 min.) and the surliest in terms of attendants. If you're going to the Hancock, park in the Esplanade Garage at 900 Lake Shore Dr. ($1.65 for 5 hrs.). Enter via ramp on Delaware immediately east of DeWitt, or use DeWitt Garage, 260 E. Chestnut (same rate).

Rush St., Old Town, Mid North, New Town, Chinatown. Street parking is practically nonexistent. Except for Chinatown (new big lot maintained by area restaurants at northeast corner Cermak & Wentworth), use cabs or CTA if you're going to restaurants or shops in any of these areas.

Bicycle Parking. Private garages in the Loop or Near North Side may charge as much as they charge for car parking—up to $4 per day. Use these city parking structures (50¢ for 12 hours): 20 S. Wacker, 535 S. State, 320 N. LaSalle, 11 W. Wacker, 259 E. Superior. There are also a private open lot at 110 E. Grand (50¢ per day) and free racks along east side of Michigan Av. between Randolph & Monroe. Bring your own chain.

Chances R restaurant, 2125 N. Clark, and Green Planet restaurant, 2470 N. Lincoln, have free parking for customers.

PAPER, SCRAP METAL, & GLASS RECLAMATION DEPOTS

The city has no interest in collection depots for cans, bottles, paper, and other salvage for recycling. Phone your neighborhood newspaper for locations maintained by private groups. Suburbs are more ecology-minded; suburban newspapers will know locations.

Glass Container Manufacturers Institute, 208 S. LaSalle, 368-0210, will help any group set up a glass reclamation program.

Continental Can Environmental Affairs Dept., 269-2400, will direct you to nearest scrap metal reclamation center.

MEDIA

Sun-Times. Liberal morning paper inclining from slightly left toward middle of the road. Carries some of the most outspoken syndicated columnists—Joseph Alsop, Art Buchwald, William Raspberry, Garry Wills. Has Bill Mauldin and Jake Burck as leading political cartoonists. Home paper for Irv Kupcinet and Ann Landers. "Two" pullout section carries "Jory Graham's City" on Fridays.

Tribune. Conservative morning paper inching from right toward middle of the road. Admirable layout of trite women's features brings in heavy advertising from posh women's shops—a great many readers buy mainly to read the ads. In fact, the *Trib* is the most complete Chicago newspaper, and for apartment, house, or job hunting, its "Classified" sections are essential.

Daily News. Marshall Field's afternoon paper with Mike Royko on the columnist list. Good foreign news coverage from its own foreign news service. Splendid political cartoons by John Fischetti, whom Easterners will remember from the defunct *New York Herald Tribune.*

Chicago Today. The *Trib's* afternoon paper. All news is capsule—in fact, so capsule that sometimes it's like getting nothing but headlines and lead paragraphs to read. Carries Tom Wicker and James Reston and some abbreviated *New York Times* stories. No weekend editions.

Daily Defender. One of the oldest black papers in the country (1905) with columnists like the Rev. Jesse L. Jackson and Charles G. Hurst. Functions as spokesman for all elements in the black community, gives detailed coverage to community events and affairs. Friday paper covers entire weekend.

Chicago Journalism Review. Monthly gadfly to the news business nationally but with much of its strongest criticism directed against Chicago dailies.

Founded by Young Turks (working members of the Chicago press) as protest against a tendency all four Establishment dailies have of edging around certain aspects of legitimate news. Good way to learn why the Establishment press does the things it does. At newsstands or by subscription, 332-3102.

Chicago Guide. A monthly listing almost all ongoing events in the city and WFMT and Channels 11 and 20 programs in entirety. Not a *Philadelphia* or *New York Magazine.* On newsstands or by subscription, 644-1900.

Reader. A first-rate, new weekly aimed primarily at college students and young comers but read by astute people of all ages who find it delivered to their high rises as lobby giveaway. Strong young writing, excellent film reviews, and super listings of jazz, blues, soul, country, folk, rock spots. For subscription, 924-6587.

Neighborhood Newspapers. The best relate well to their communities and are comprehensive in neighborhood political news coverage. All try for paid subscriptions, but most people pick up giveaway copies in local shops and highrise lobbies.

Suburban Newspapers. You don't have to look for them—their subscription departments will find you.

Ethnic and Foreign Language Newspapers. Find some 65-70 of these listed under "Newspapers" in *Yellow Pages B.*

Townsfolk. A monthly that chronicles the comings and goings of the area's society types. Mainly by subscription but also at Field's book department.

New York Times. Chicago subscribers number 75,000. Daily editions can be found at leading hotels and newsstands on the Near North Side. Also at newsstands in major Loop office buildings. Sunday airmail edition has far broader city-suburban distribution. Phone *Times* ad office, RA 6-3300, for nearest location.

Wall Street Journal. Chicago edition is practically identical to editions published in New York, Dallas, San Francisco. On newsstands or by subscription, 648-7681.

Underground Press. It's fluid but you can always find copies of its leading newspapers at head and phonograph shops and offbeat bookstores. *Seed,* published here, 929-0133, is also hawked on State St.

Post Office News, 37 W. Monroe, RA 6-4386, carries airmail editions of British, German, Italian, French, etc., newspapers and magazines. Also one-month back issues of U.S. magazines.

Newsstand on northwest corner of State & Washington carries out-of-town papers from all over the U.S. So does a stand at Quincy & State and Main Street Newsstand (Main & Chicago) in Evanston.

Library of International Relations, 660 N. Wabash, is crammed with current newspapers, journals, magazines from more than 100 nations.

TV Stations

WBBM-TV (CBS) Ch. 2	WGN-TV Ch. 9	WCIU-TV Ch. 26
WMAQ-TV (NBC) Ch. 5	WTTW Ch. 11	WFLD Ch. 32
WLS-TV (ABC) Ch. 7	WXXW Ch. 20	WSNS Ch. 44

Channel 11 is Chicago's Public Broadcasting Service station. The best of PBS is very good indeed but local WTTW efforts are often dismal. Channels 26, 32, 44 are UHF.

Radio Stations. Don't be surprised if a station changes its format—change is an industry neurosis. **MOR** is the acronym for middle-of-the-road. Radio uses the term to describe the kind of music that doesn't offend anyone. **Talk** means stations that invite audience phone-in. **Fine Arts** programming means classical music, drama, discussion, news.

AM Stations
>**All News:** WBBM/780
>**Rock/MOR/Talk:** WIND/560; WMAQ/670
>**MOR/Talk:** WGN/720; WIVS/850
>**MOR:** WAIT/820; WNUS/1390; WEEF/1430
>**Top 40:** WLS/890; WCFL/1000
>**Rhythm & Blues:** WGRT/950
>**Jazz:** WBEE/1570
>**Country & Western:** WJJD/1160
>**Foreign Language:** WOPA/1490
>**Black Radio:** WVON/1450

FM Stations
>**Fine Arts:** WNIB/97.1; WFMT/98.7
>**Country & Western:** WJJD-FM/104.3
>**Progressive Rock:** WDAI/94.7; WBBM-FM/96.3; WGLD-FM/102.7
>**Rock/Jazz:** WSDM/97.9
>**Rock:** WMAQ-FM/101.1
>**Classical/MOR/Contemporary:** WXFM/105.9
>**MOR:** WWMM/92.7; WLAK/93.9; WRMN-FM/94.3; WDHF-FM/95.5; WFMF/100.3; WCLR-FM/101.9; WEFA/102.3; WEEF-FM/103.1; WKFM/103.5; WNUS-FM/107.5
>**All Foreign Language:** WXRT-FM/93.1
>**Chicago Board of Education:** WBEZ/91.5
>**News/MOR from '30s & '40s:** WVFV/103.9
>**University Stations:** WHPK/88.3, U. of C. station (can be picked up consistently only on South Side)—classical, jazz, folk, rock, underground, discussions; WNUR-FM/89.3, N.U. station (reaches Chicago on clear nights with strong wind)—classical, jazz, folk, rock, underground, discussions

INFORMATION CENTER

Information Center, Chicago Public Library, Randolph & Michigan, CE 6-8922, Ext. 231-235. Competent staff of 14 at this phone-in–drop-by center (in main Reference Dept.) gives quick, accurate answers on any subject or tells you where to go to find answer. Has 900-volume reference library at its fingertips plus all files from defunct *Tribune* Public Information Center. Open 9 AM-9 PM Mon.-Fri., 9 AM-5:30 PM Sat.

THEATRES

Blackstone, 60 E. Balbo, CE 6-8240
Studebaker, 418 S. Michigan, 922-2973
Shubert, 22 W. Monroe, CE 6-8240
Civic Theatre, 20 N. Wacker, FI 6-0270
Goodman Memorial Theatre, 200 S. Columbus Dr., CE 6-2337
Ivanhoe, 3000 N. Clark, 248-6800
Forum, 5620 S. Harlem, Summit, 496-3000
Arlington Park, 3400 W. Euclid, Arlington Heights, 392-6800

DINNER THEATRES

Drury Lane, 2500 W. 94th Pl., Evergreen Park, PR 9-4000
Candlelight Dinner Playhouse, 5620 S. Harlem, Summit, GL 8-7373
In the Round Dinner Playhouse, 6072 S. Archer, 581-3090
Country Club Theatre, Old Orchard Country Club, Rand & Euclid, Mount Prospect, 259-5400
Pheasant Run Playhouse, Pheasant Run Lodge, Rte. 64, St. Charles, 584-1454 or Chicago number 261-7943

CABARET, COMMUNITY, COLLEGE, & CHILDREN'S THEATRES

See "Weekender Guide," *Sun-Times.*

CONCERTS & OPERA

Orchestra Hall, 216 S. Michigan, 427-7711 (Chicago Symphony Orchestra)
Civic Opera House, 20 N. Wacker, FI 6-0270 (Lyric Opera)
Auditorium, 70 E. Congress, 922-2110
Ravinia Pavilion, Ravinia Park, south end of Highland Park, ST 2-9696 or box office 273-3500 (summer home Chicago Symphony Orchestra)
Grant Park Music Shell, 11th St. between Columbus Dr. & Lake Shore Dr., HA 7-5252

MAJOR MUSEUMS

Hours change from summer to winter—phone. For full museum descriptions, see *Chicago: An Extraordinary Guide* by Jory Graham (Rand McNally).

Art Institute of Chicago, Adams & Michigan, CE 6-7080. Daily. You don't have to pay, but Art Institute suggests: adults $1; children, senior citizens 50¢; asks no money on Thurs.

Field Museum of Natural History, Roosevelt Rd. & Lake Shore Dr., 922-9410. Daily. Adults $1; children 6-17, students, senior citizens 35¢; families $2.50; free on Fri.

Adler Planetarium, 1300 S. Lake Shore Dr. (Northerly Island), 294-4620. Daily. Museum free. Sky show: adults $1; under 18, 50¢.

John G. Shedd Aquarium, 1200 S. Lake Shore Dr. (Roosevelt), WE 9-2426. Daily except Christmas and New Year's. Adults $1; families $2.50; to age 17, 35¢; free on Fri.

Museum of Science and Industry, 57th St. & South Shore Dr., MU 4-1414. Daily. Free.

Chicago Academy of Sciences, 2001 N. Clark, LI 9-0606. Daily. Free.

Museum of Contemporary Art, 237 E. Ontario, 943-7755. Daily. Adults $1; students 50¢; under 6 free.

Oriental Institute, 1155 E. 58th, 753-2471. Closed Mon., holidays. Free.

Chicago Historical Society, North Av. & Clark St., MI 2-4600. Daily. Adults 50¢; ages 6-17, senior citizens 25¢; families $1. Mon. free (or Tues. if Mon. is holiday).

WORTHWHILE, NOT MAJOR, MUSEUMS

Lizzadro Museum of Lapidary Art, 220 Cottage Hill (Wilder Park), Elmhurst, 833-1616. Closed Mon. Adults 50¢; ages 13-18, 25¢; free under 13; free on Fri.

DuSable Museum of African-American History, 3806 S. Michigan, 624-8121. Closed Mon. Adults 50¢; students, children 25¢.

Maurice Spertus Museum of Judaica, College of Jewish Studies, 72 E. 11th, 922-9012. Closed Fri., Sat. Free.

Jane Addams Hull House, Halsted & Polk, 996-2793. Daily. Free.

ZOOS & BOTANICA

Lincoln Park Zoo, between Webster & Fullerton, along Lincoln Park West, 549-3000. Daily. Free.

Brookfield Zoo, 8400 W. 31st, Brookfield, BI 2-2630. Daily. Adults $1; under 15, 25¢ (free when accompanied by adult); free on Tues.

Morton Arboretum, intersection of East-West Tollway and Ill. 53, Lisle, WO 8-0074. Daily. Parking, including admission, $1.

Botanic Garden, Dundee Rd., just east of Edens Expy in Glencoe, 835-5360. Daily but closed weekends mid-October to May. Free.

Lincoln Park Conservatory, Stockton Dr. at 2300 N., LI 9-3006. Daily. Free.

Garfield Park Conservatory, 300 N. Central Park at Lake St., KE 3-1281. Daily. Free.

SPORTS ARENAS

Chicago Stadium, 1800 W. Madison, 733-5300

Soldier Field Stadium, 425 E. 14th, HA 7-5252

Wrigley Field, Addison & Clark, 281-5050

White Sox Park, 324 W. 35th, 924-1000

International Amphitheatre, 43rd & Halsted, 927-5580

Dyche Stadium, 1501 Central, Evanston, 492-7070

Oak Brook International Sports Core (Polo), 1000 Oak Brook Rd., Oak Brook, 654-2211

RACETRACKS

Arlington Park, Northwest Hwy & Wilke Rd., Arlington Heights, CL 5-4300

Hawthorne, 3501 S. Laramie, Cicero, 242-1350

Maywood Park, North Av. & 5th St., Maywood, MA 6-4816

Sportsman's Park, 3301 S. Laramie, Cicero, BI 2-1121

Washington Park, 175th & Halsted, Homewood, SY 8-1700

USEFUL PUBLICATIONS

Legislative Directory. A guide to current Chicago, Cook County, Illinois public officials and where to reach them. Also membership of Illinois Senate and House of Representatives and their standing committees; all elected executive officers; and maps of wards, state senatorial districts, U.S. House of Representatives districts. From Assn. of Commerce & Industry, $3.15.

Illinois Voter's Handbook. Helps voters understand local political structure and government. Published by League of Women Voters, 67 E. Madison, $2.25.

CHAPTER IV

HELP—MEDICAL

HOW TO FIND A DOCTOR

Because of the shortage of physicians, if you're not somebody's patient before you get sick, you're unlikely to become his patient when you need him most. Top physicians in private practice are rarely available to nonpatients on instant demand—at least not in large metropolitan centers.*

The physician † you first want is a primary-care physician—a specialist in internal medicine. He takes initial responsibility for all your medical problems, and if there's one he can't handle, he'll refer you to another specialist who can. You call a primary-care physician if you have flu or one of the innumerable viruses or if you break your arm and need referral to an orthopedic specialist. Because a primary-care physician specializes in internal medicine, he's often referred to as an internist—not to be confused with an intern, who is a graduate medical student in further training to become a licensed MD.

If you're from out of town, ask your former MD for names he can recommend here. Top men know each other through national medical societies.

If you didn't arrive with names and must start cold, ask the switchboard operator at any of the principal teaching hospitals (p. 61-63) to connect you with the department that handles referrals. Ask for names of primary-care physicians. Be frank about the qualities you like in a physician—candor, responsiveness, or whatever. If you know you need a gynecologist or obstetrician, a pediatrician, psychiatrist, urologist, or other specialist, follow the same procedure.

Reason for phoning a teaching hospital: in a city the size of Chicago, with all kinds of hospitals, some topnotch, some not, the principal teaching hospitals are where you generally find the most capable staff physicians—the ones who are really up on current diagnosis and treatment because they are teaching.†† Furthermore, a major teaching hospital always has a medical house staff (interns and residents) that tends to keep the senior men on their toes.

To find a specialist in the suburbs, use the list of hospitals on p. 63-64

---

* If you don't believe it's hard to find a doctor when you need one desperately, read "How To Pick a Doctor," Michael Halberstam, MD, New York Magazine, June 14, 1971, or "Where Have Our Doctors Gone?" Jack Star, Look, June 29, 1971. Mr. Star, then a Look senior editor, lives with his family in Park Forest. His four-day search for a doctor when he had double pneumonia will convince you of the absolute necessity of becoming a patient before you're ill.

† Other than an obstetrician-gynecologist or pediatrician.

†† A teaching hospital has in-depth training programs in all departments.

and ask the switchboard operator to connect you with the department that handles referrals. Procedure here is the same as at teaching hospitals. Or call your county medical society for referrals.

Hospital residents are in an excellent position to know the most competent, most humane, most communicative specialists at their hospital. Though you can't very well walk into an emergency room and hang around waiting to collar a resident, if you're in an emergency room for one reason or another, that's the time to ask.

You can also call **Chicago Medical Society,** 310 S. Michigan, 922-0417, for its MD referral service (Cook County only). Women on the switchboard will give names of three physicians in your community who are members of CMS —general practitioners, internists, other specialists. Referral hours are 9:30 AM-4:30 PM, Mon.-Fri. The switchboard is always jammed. Hence, call only when you've time to see if you like a doctor (as for a checkup) but not in a crisis. If you've an emergency, get to a hospital emergency room.

If you'd feel happier with someone like the old family doctor, who can treat infections, set a simple fracture, give the kids their shots, look for a physician specializing in family practice. Family practice as a specialty is so new it's only beginning to appear in teaching hospitals, but almost 900 physicians in the Chicago area are now family-practice specialists. Locate through Chicago Medical Society.

To find a dentist, call Chicago Dental Society, 30 N. Michigan, RA 6-4076. Ask for names of two or three dentists in your ZIP Code area. The Society can direct you to children's dentists, general dentists, and specialists in Cook, Lake, and Du Page Counties, prefers to send you to a generalist first since you may have incorrectly diagnosed your woes. Society also maintains a Wednesday List of dentists who have Wednesday office hours.

For a serious late-night, weekend, or holiday dental emergency, when you don't know anyone, see special emergency services at Presbyterian-St. Luke's Hospital, p. 62; Billings Hospital (a University of Chicago hospital), p. 63; Evanston Hospital, p. 62.

To find a psychiatrist or psychoanalyst, call the switchboard of a teaching hospital or the Institute for Psychoanalysis, 180 N. Michigan, 726-6300 (p. 71).

IN AN EMERGENCY

By law, no Chicago hospital can turn any patient away from its emergency room. However, some emergency rooms haven't been worthy of the name.

Partly as a way of letting little hospitals with inadequate resources opt out of trying to provide major emergency room care and partly to use emergency resources more efficiently, Illinois, by law, requires all hospitals to classify their emergency rooms as to the kind of care they're able to give.

The classification system is complicated and not resolved as this book goes to press. Furthermore, since this is a pioneer venture, the system isn't going to be perfect instantly.

At present, if you live in Chicago and have to deal with a critical emergency, have no physician to turn to, and don't know what kind of care you can get in a nearby hospital emergency room—head for the emergency room at one of the hospitals on p. 61-63. For the most part, they're the principal teaching hospitals for the big medical schools in the Chicago area, and their emergency rooms have always been geared to general emergency care of the best kind available.

Emergency room care isn't free. Get in the habit of carrying your health insurance card or a checkbook—all the time. Chicago hospitals are getting very hard on people who can't pay for emergency room treatment. Some will literally ship you in a police squadrol to Cook County Hospital for treatment there. Squadrols have no lifesaving equipment of any kind; nor will anyone in the squadrol attend you.

Current minimum emergency room fees are $15-25. If you've no cash and no health insurance card, you might as well head for Cook County Hospital in the first place.

Cook County Hospital (p. 62) is for people with no money and no health insurance card. It scarcely looks like the hospital in TV's "Medical Center," but it gives good medical care. For burns and trauma (severe physical injury caused by auto or other accident, gunshot, stabbing, beating), Cook County Hospital is *the* place to go regardless.

If you live in the suburbs, use emergency rooms at hospitals on p. 63-64.

Illinois ER (Emergency Room) Classification System. Hospital ERs are rated in three categories solely on the basis of service they're able to give.

Comprehensive. Defines an ER with a licensed physician* on duty on a 24-hour basis and specialists in internal medicine, obstetrics-gynecology, surgery, and pediatrics available within minutes. (The law doesn't specify how many minutes.) Certain subspecialists must also be available within minutes— a plastic surgeon, an ophthalmologist, etc. Comprehensive ERs must also have 24-hour ancillary services necessary to patient care—labs, X ray, electrocardiogram (EKG) equipment, pharmacy, blood bank, and the like.

Basic. Defines an ER with a licensed physician* on duty on a 24-hour basis and specialists in internal medicine, surgery, pediatrics, and obstetrics-gynecology available within minutes. (Again minutes is not defined.) Ancillary services may be in hospital or on call. This can make a difference—if you need an immediate blood transfusion, for instance.

Standby. Defines an ER with a registered nurse on duty. Nurses are being trained to sustain life until a patient can be transferred by ambulance to a Basic or Comprehensive emergency room—or if this is your hospital, until your physician can get to you.

One advantage of the classification system: you won't necessarily have to rush miles to a principal teaching hospital for emergency room care. A Comprehensive or Basic emergency room may be much nearer—and equally practical. Again, the one exception is trauma—unless you're closer to a state-designated trauma center (see below), head for Cook County Hospital (p. 62).

---

* Physician can be a hospital resident.

To learn how emergency rooms at your nearest hospitals are classified, phone or write **Division of Emergency Medical Services, Illinois Dept. of Public Health,** 3rd Floor West, Cook County Hospital, 1835 W. Harrison, 60612. Phone 793-3880.

Unfortunately, the city sometimes uses the designations Class A, Class B, Class C for Comprehensive, Basic, and Standby emergency rooms—confusing.

Expect any emergency room to be jammed; these days, everyone who can't find a doctor heads for one. Expect to wait—especially if your problem is one that can wait. At least 80% of all people who fill emergency rooms aren't emergencies; 15% fall into the category of emergency but not life-and-death critical; 5% are indeed critical. You can be sophisticated about emergency room treatment; with a serious problem, ask the resident who examines you to call in a staff specialist.

Trauma Centers officially designated at this time by the state are: Cook County Hospital and Children's Memorial Hospital (for children to age 16) in Chicago (p. 70); Evanston Hospital, Evanston; Foster G. McGaw Hospital, Maywood; Christ Community Hospital, Oak Lawn; St. Therese Hospital, Waukegan; Memorial Hospital of DuPage County, Elmhurst; St. Joseph Hospital, Joliet (for suburban hospitals, see p. 63-64).

Wesley Pavilion (see below) at Northwestern Memorial Hospital, Chicago, is an officially designated Spinal Cord Trauma Center.

Large blue-and-white signs on federal highways in the metropolitan area stating "Trauma Center" direct you to the above. The signs really have even greater significance downstate, where they supply a systematic way of getting someone critically injured to a good hospital.

LEADING HOSPITALS
(For leading pediatric hospitals, see p. 70-71.)

Near North Side to Evanston

Northwestern Memorial Hospital, Superior St. & Fairbanks Ct. (two blocks east of Michigan Av.). This is the new name for two of Northwestern University medical school's principal teaching hospitals across the street from each other on Superior.

Passavant Pavilion (formerly Passavant Memorial Hospital), 649-3000. Emergency room on Fairbanks Ct.

Wesley Pavilion (formerly Chicago Wesley Memorial Hospital), 649-2000. Emergency room on Superior St. Official state-designated Spinal Cord Trauma Center, 649-3425

St. Joseph's Hospital, 2900 N. Lake Shore Dr., 528-1000. Teaching hospital for Loyola University school of medicine. Emergency entrance at rear of hospital on Commonwealth—enter from Surf or Diversey.

Louis A. Weiss Memorial Hospital, 4646 N. Marine Dr., UP 8-8700. Teaching hospital for University of Illinois medical school. General emergency care. Emergency entrance, corner Clarendon & Leland.

Evanston Hospital, 2650 Ridge, Evanston, 492-2000. Teaching hospital for

Northwestern University medical school. Official state-designated trauma center. Emergency entrance at north end of hospital on Ridge. Emergency services include:

> **Poison Control Center,** 492-6460. Advice by phone, immediate hospitalization when necessary.
>
> **Dental Emergency Service,** 492-6460. Similar to Presbyterian-St. Luke's below.
>
> **Trauma & Burn Units,** 492-6460

West to Maywood

Presbyterian-St. Luke's Hospital, 1753 W. Congress, 942-5000. Principal teaching hospital for Rush University school of medicine. Emergency entrance on Congress near Wood. Emergency services include:

> **Poison Control Center,** 942-5969. Advice by phone, immediate hospital treatment when necessary.
>
> **Dental Emergency Unit,** 942-6330. Competent dental intern on duty at all times, staff oral surgeons and other dental specialists on call. Phone first. Also be sure emergency is genuine—not a mere toothache but a complication like a suspected abscess or tooth broken off at gum line.

University of Illinois Hospital (formerly U. of I. Research & Education Hospital), 840 S. Wood, 996-7000. Principal teaching hospital for the U. of I. school of medicine. Emergency entrance at rear. Use driveway south of main entrance.

Mount Sinai Hospital Medical Center, 2750 W. 15th Pl., 542-2000. Principal teaching hospital for Chicago Medical School. Emergency entrance at end of block on W. 15th St. Emergency services include:

> **Poison Control Center,** 542-2030

Cook County Hospital, 1835 W. Harrison, 633-6100. Teaching hospital for University of Illinois, Northwestern University, Loyola University. Official state-designated trauma center. Emergency entrance at back of hospital between Harrison and Polk.

> **Burn Unit,** 633-6564. World-famous for its comprehensive treatment of burns.
>
> **Trauma Unit,** 633-6040. For accidents of all kinds—gunshot and knife wounds, heavy bleeding, massive external and suspected internal injuries. Intensive care, immediate surgery if needed. Rate $110 per day regardless of injury or number of services given. Policy is to treat first, handle financing later. If you've no insurance and no money, financing can be arranged.

Foster G. McGaw Hospital (new name for Loyola University Hospital), 2160 S. First Av., Maywood, 531-3000. Official state-designated trauma center. Emergency entrance at rear of building near 12th St. Emergency services include:

> **Poison Control Center,** 531-3882
>
> **Burn Unit,** 531-3986
>
> **Trauma Unit,** 531-3886 or switchboard

South Side

Mercy Hospital, 2520 S. Prairie, VI 2-4700. Teaching hospital for University of Illinois. Emergency entrance, 26th & Indiana.

Michael Reese Hospital & Medical Center, 29th at Ellis, 791-2000. Teaching hospital affiliated with University of Chicago school of medicine. Emergency entrance at Mandel Clinic, 29th & Vernon.

University of Chicago Hospitals & Clinics, 950 E. 59th, 947-1000. Teaching hospitals for U. of C. Staff physicians are full-time members of the medical faculty, see patients only at hospital clinics—the equivalent of private physicians' offices. No free clinic care. Emergency entrance in Billings Hospital at south end of private drive (past parking lot)—access from 58th & Drexel. Emergency services include:

> **Poison Control Center,** 947-6231
>
> **Dental Emergency Care,** 947-5691. Similar to Presbyterian-St. Luke's (p. 62).
>
> **Transfusion Component Service for Hemophiliacs,** 947-5579
>
> **Kidney Dialysis Unit,** 947-5801. Two weeks' notice for visitors to Chicago.

South Chicago Community Hospital, 2320 E. 93rd, 978-2000. Emergency entrance at 92nd Pl. & Oglesby. Not a teaching hospital but best facility on far South Side.

MEDICAL SCHOOL & HOSPITAL CLINICS

All medical schools or their affiliated hospitals maintain outpatient treatment facilities—clinics. Example: Northwestern University's medical school maintains clinics in all specialties from Allergies and Dentistry through High Cholesterol and Psychiatry. Team treatment by hospital residents and medical students under the direction of a faculty specialist. Phone admitting office for appointment Mon.-Fri., 8 AM-4 PM, 747 Fairbanks Ct., 649-8118.

All clinics expect you to pay for services, either in cash or with a health insurance card or public aid card. Fees may vary according to ability to pay.

SUBURBAN HOSPITALS

Arlington Heights	Northwest Community Hospital, 800 W. Central Rd., 259-1000
Blue Island	St. Francis Hospital, 12935 S. Gregory, 597-2000
Chicago Heights	St. James Hospital, 1423 Chicago Rd., 756-1000
Des Plaines	Holy Family Hospital, 100 N. River Rd., 297-1800
Elgin	Sherman Hospital, 934 Center, 742-9800
Elk Grove Village	Alexian Brothers Medical Center, 800 W. Biesterfield Rd., 437-5500
Elmhurst	Memorial Hospital of DuPage County, 209 Avon Rd., 833-1400; official state-designated trauma center
Evanston	Evanston Hospital, 2650 Ridge, 492-2000. See p. 61.
	St. Francis Hospital, 355 Ridge, 492-4000

Evergreen Park	Little Company of Mary Hospital, 2800 W. 95th, 422-6200
Geneva	Community Hospital, 416 S. Second St., CE 2-0771
Harvey	Ingalls Memorial Hospital, 15510 Page, 333-2300
Highland Park	Highland Park Hospital, 718 Glenview Av., 432-8000
Hinsdale	Hinsdale Sanitarium & Hospital, 120 N. Oak, 323-2100
Joliet	St. Joseph Hospital, 333 N. Madison, 815-725-7133; official state-designated trauma center
La Grange	Community Memorial General Hospital, 5101 Willow Springs Rd., 352-1200
Lake Forest	Lake Forest Hospital, 660 N. Westmoreland Rd., 234-5600
Libertyville	Condell Memorial Hospital, Cleveland & Stewart Avs., 362-2900
Maywood	Foster G. McGaw Hospital, 2160 S. First Av., 531-3000. See p. 62.
Melrose Park	Gottlieb Memorial Hospital, 8700 W. North, 681-3200
Naperville	Edward Hospital, S. Washington St., 355-0450
Oak Lawn	Christ Community Hospital, 4440 W. 95th, 425-8000; official state-designated trauma center
Oak Park	West Suburban Hospital, 518 N. Austin Blvd., 383-6200
Oak Park-Berwyn	MacNeal Memorial Hospital, 3249 S. Oak Park Av., 797-3000
Palos Heights	Palos Heights Community Hospital, 123rd St. & 80th Av., 361-4500
Park Ridge	Lutheran General Hospital, 1775 Dempster, 696-2210
St. Charles	Delnor Hospital, 975 N. Fifth, 584-3300
Skokie	Skokie Valley Community Hospital, 9600 Gross Point Rd., 677-9600
Waukegan	St. Therese Hospital, 2615 Washington, 688-5800; official state-designated trauma center
Winfield	Central DuPage Hospital, 0 North 025 Winfield Rd., 653-6900
Woodstock	Memorial Hospital for McHenry County, 527 W. South St., 815-338-2500

SUICIDE PREVENTION & PSYCHIATRIC EMERGENCIES

A psychiatric emergency is one in which you—or anyone else—might harm yourself or another person. It's also the kind of emotional crisis that makes you feel you're losing control.

Suicide isn't the only way out. Somewhere in Chicago there are people who know your life is worthwhile. Get to the emergency room at a teaching hospital or phone and ask the switchboard to connect you with a psychiatric resident.

Michael Reese Hospital Dept. of Psychiatry, 791-2050, is especially helpful. This phone is a 24-hour emergency phone, and a psychiatric resident is on duty at all times. Fee based on sliding scale.

Community hospitals are beginning to be funded by the state to provide crisis intervention. **Ravenswood Hospital Medical Center,** 4550 N. Winchester, has a 24-hour traveling psychiatric team that goes out to rescue a person who's so suicidal or in such a state of crisis he can't get to a hospital. Area limited: 2800-5600 north, 1800 west to North Branch of Chicago River. Crisis phone 769-6200.

Kool-Aide (p. 67) offers good nonmedical crisis help to students, drop-outs, the young. Staff trained in suicide prevention, knows what it's doing.

SPECIAL HELP FOR STUDENTS:
VD, DRUGS, CRISIS INTERVENTION, PREGNANCY

Everyone has his own fantasy about what a good doctor should be. Almost nobody wants a physician who moralizes. However, when your body needs competent medical care, forget about an MD's personality and go get help.

If you live near the pediatrician who took care of you when you were little, call him. If you're a girl with a vaginal infection or if you think you're pregnant or if you're afraid you have VD, go to your mother's gynecologist—he'll help. Be sure to tell him what you're worried about, especially if you think you have VD. If you merely say you have an infection, he isn't likely to think you mean VD. Worse, in examining you, he won't examine for VD. He'll look for an infection as commonplace as a yeast infection—and if he finds one, that's what he'll treat—not VD.

VD. Illinois law protects minors who have or think they have syphilis or gonorrhea—GC, the clap. All records of diagnosis and treatment are confidential. No parent is notified unless a minor is under age 12.

For free treatment in hospital clinic nearest you, phone **Francis Juvenile Home Assn.,** 726-0982. Age limit is 19, but nobody asks for your birth certificate (neither does anyone at Board of Health clinics). You're merely asked for your name and the area you live in so that the nearest hospital clinic knows you're coming in for free treatment. The sole purpose of this private nonprofit corporation is to help you. It's the kind of place you can phone and say, "I'm 14 and I'm afraid I have the clap and I'm scared." All records kept confidential.

The Chicago Board of Health runs two walk-in VD clinics where examination, treatment, and follow-up are free. The clinics aren't princely, but they're staffed by competent doctors who won't turn you off. Use your head —give names of sexual partners when asked for them. VD is a raging epidemic and has to be stopped. People who heal you at clinics below know how to deal tactfully and in confidence with anyone you've slept with.

Municipal Social Hygiene Clinic, 27 E. 26th, VI 2-0222

Herman N. Bundesen District Health Center, 100 N. Central Park (in Garfield Park, in building with dome), 638-3365

Drug Overdose & Drug Poisoning. In any drug-related medical emergency except a bad trip or heroin addiction, take the risk of a report by the cop who may be on duty in the emergency room and get your friend whose life is on the line to one of the hospitals listed below. All have specially trained their emergency room staffs to deal with overdose and drug poisoning, like barbiturate overdose, any combination of barbiturates with alcohol, or LSD cut, say, with strychnine.

Illinois Masonic Hospital, 834 W. Wellington, 525-2300. Emergency entrance next to main entrance.

Presbyterian-St. Luke's Hospital (p. 62)

Passavant Pavilion (p. 61)

Ravenswood Hospital, 4550 N. Winchester, 878-4300. Emergency entrance at rear of hospital.

American Hospital, 850 W. Irving Park, LA 5-6780. Emergency entrance next to main entrance.

Henrotin Hospital, 111 W. Oak, 943-5500. Emergency entrance on LaSalle. Cash or a health insurance card is essential. Lacking either, call **Pflash Tyre,** 549-8388, for medical referral to nearest free neighborhood clinic.

Illinois Drug Abuse Program (IDAP). The state works with the University of Chicago to operate IDAP, a flexible drug treatment effort. Staff includes ex-addicts, is sympathetic, and has savvy. IDAP Chicago headquarters is the major resource for information about drugs, drug abuse, drug-related problems, and treatment centers. Phone Office of Public Information, 955-9800, Mon.-Fri., 9 AM-5 PM, or use hot line, 955-3929.

Forest Hospital, 555 Wilson, Des Plaines, 827-8811. A psychiatric hospital that also treats acute and chronic drug users and alcoholics. Has outpatient methadone clinic sponsored by IDAP. Treats drug situations like intoxication, flashback, withdrawal, bad trips—but not those that are life-threatening and require emergency room facilities and staff (hospital has no emergency room).

Alternatives, Inc., 2550 W. Peterson, 973-5400; hot line after 2 PM, 973-5404. The most ambitious, comprehensive program in the city, community-based and partially funded by IDAP. Staffed by hip professionals, ex-users, and young people of high school age. Primarily designed to serve the northeast section of Chicago but will handle nonmedical emergencies from all areas. Sends rescue squad if necessary. No fees and no red tape. Main business: to develop real alternatives to drugs; for instance, training in broadcast skills with programs aired on WNIB-FM. Also provides information on all aspects of drug use; drug analysis service; training for crisis intervention work. Operates two storefront outposts:

Rogers Park Center, 1537 W. Morse, 465-3572. Drug rescue help plus music learning exchange.

Edgewater Outpost, 5866 N. Broadway, 275-1076. Drug rescue help plus theatre group, ecology projects.

Pflash Tyre Company-Illinois Drug Abuse Program, 2127 N. Kenmore; 24-hour hot line, 549-8388. A major, free facility, both residential (ages 13-20) and outpatient (ages 13-25). Crisis intervention, polydrug abuse treatment (except heroin), barbiturate detoxification help through hospitals; individual and group treatment, recreational programs: poetry workshop, free theatre, free school, arts and crafts. Also parents' group and family therapy. Professional staff—consulting psychiatrist, psychologists, psychiatric nurses—as well as ex-addict staff. Ex-addict staff has been through treatment.

Kool-Aide, 30 W. Chicago (in Lawson YMCA), 664-0505. Emergency rescue service for bad trips and crises. Counseling with emphasis on referral (and follow-up) to agencies this volunteer cooperative knows are sympathetic and effective. Choices are excellent. So is Kool-Aide staff, which includes a number of graduates in psychology and mental health. Not affiliated with IDAP.

HELP, 2210 N. Halsted; 24-hour hot line, 929-5150. HELP is trying to be the central emergency switchboard for city and suburbs, is currently tied in with 15 up-to-date and accountable crisis centers including Pflash Tyre and Alternatives. Rescue squads available around the clock—nobody left stranded. Partially funded by Playboy.

Suburban Hot Lines & Drop-in Centers. Locate the most reliable through HELP, IDAP, Alternatives.

Looking Glass, 1968 W. Wilson, 334-2601. Good place to go if you've split from your family. Professional staff is realistic, sympathetic—knows about cooling-off needs. Police won't hassle you here.

Grace Church Youth Help Center, 555 W. Belden, 929-3553. Volunteer organization with a young staff gives help with similar problems.

Heroin. Call **IDAP Drug Abuse Information Line,** 955-3929, for referral to clinic nearest you. Treatment usually includes outpatient methadone clinic, individual counseling, peer group therapy. Treatment generally free or minimal weekly fee.

Pregnancy. If you're pregnant, use your head and see your doctor or gynecologist as soon as possible. If you want to have your baby, arrangements must be made. There are very few good facilities in this city for girls who must leave home to have their babies—you have to get on a waiting list. If you don't know a doctor, call one of the following for referral and for help having the baby:

> **Illinois Children's Home & Aid Society, Maternity Unit,** 1122 N. Dearborn, WH 4-3313.
>
> **Crittenton Comprehensive Care Center,** 3639 S. Michigan, 268-6120, or 4257 W. Washington, 826-3900.
>
> **Salvation Army Family Service Division,** 10 E. Pearson, 944-0378, or its Community Counseling Service, 1797 Oakton, Des Plaines, 827-7191.

At Crittenton and Salvation Army homes, you're sheltered, you're with girls who are also pregnant, you're kept busy in healthy ways—can even go to school—you get good counseling, good medical care, the best kind of help placing the baby or arranging for adoption.

ABORTION

The swiftness of the Supreme Court decision legalizing abortion caught hospitals unready. Medical staffs were suddenly confronted with innumerable problems to solve, decisions to make. In May 1973, they were still trying to plan facilities for outpatients and for inpatients (24-hour stay).

At this time, no Chicago-area hospital knows how many abortions it can handle in a week. Hence, each is restricting admissions until it discovers what's possible.

Roman Catholic hospitals have stated they will not perform abortions at all.

To get an abortion in a hospital, phone your obstetrician-gynecologist. If you don't know one, use the procedure for locating a specialist on p. 58. Current fees: $125-150 for surgery. With hospitalization, total expenses can be as high as $450. See if your health insurance card covers some part of your costs.

If you're an unmarried minor, you'll need parental consent. If you're married, some hospitals may insist upon your husband's consent.

Note: Cook County Hospital permits abortions regardless of your age, ability to pay, or place of residence. Abortions free to women on public aid, cost up to $150 on a sliding scale for women who can pay something. A counseling session and medical examination are required before surgery.

Planned Parenthood, 185 N. Wabash, 726-5134; Abortion Referral, 726-5166. Beautiful help from a service organization that neither sells abortions nor makes judgments. The following are free if you've no funds at all; otherwise, sliding scale fitted to income:

Information on pregnancy testing services

Abortion counseling in small groups and individually

Abortion referral to Chicago and New York hospitals and qualified clinics. Currently, you may be able to get an abortion faster and less expensively in New York than in Chicago simply because New York has been set up for abortions so much longer. Abortion fees in New York start at $125.

Referrals for having your baby, adoptions, etc.

Contraceptive devices available to anyone over age 13

VD testing

Vasectomy*

Teen Scene. Referral for pregnancy testing, rap sessions, counseling.

Evanston-North Shore Health Dept. Family Planning Clinic, 1806 Maple, Evanston, GR 5-3100, Ext. 337. One of the few suburban clinics (others are in Des Plaines and Bellwood) to offer pregnancy testing, abortion referral and to prescribe birth control aids. By appointment only, long waiting list.

RAPE

If you've been raped—regardless of the hour—phone your gynecologist immediately, let him send you to his hospital.

If you don't know a gynecologist, call your primary-care physician.

If you don't know any physician who can refer you to a gynecologist, go to the nearest hospital emergency room and ask for an immediate examination. Try to phone ahead—ask if a resident in gynecology can meet you on arrival. If calling the police to take you to a hospital is the fast way to get there, call them. A police report is essential, but if it's easier to call the police after you get to an emergency room, do it then.

---

*Also available through Midwest Population Center, 100 E. Ohio, 644-3410; sliding fee to $150 based on ability to pay.

The reason for immediacy is to establish proof of sperm. It's extremely difficult to prove a rape charge in Illinois; you want all possible evidence on hospital and police records.* So, even though your first instinct after rape is to bathe and change clothes—don't. Just as a medical examination can prove intercourse, so the condition of your clothes may help indicate use of force.

Again, if you've come into an emergency room cold, ask the resident who examines you to give you the name of the best gynecologist on the staff and ask him to help you get a next-day appointment. A gynecologist will examine you for any internal injuries. He can also do what the hospital won't do—prevent pregnancy and give you VD tests. Be sure to ask for these. Pregnancy can be prevented in several ways, say with a large dosage of an estrogen or simple surgery—a D&C (dilatation and curettage). A D&C hospitalizes you 24-48 hours at most.

Women who've been raped know the humiliation of having to prove it. Hospitals traditionally treat your physical problems but ignore the psychological ones. If you're a rape victim and can possibly get to the emergency room at Billings Hospital, 950 E. 59th (a University of Chicago hospital), go there. Physicians in this emergency room are noted for a more compassionate attitude toward rape victims; in addition, you'll get help from a university chaplain trained in crisis intervention.

Planned Parenthood, 726-5134, also offers free counseling after rape— gives you the chance to sort out your feelings and cope with the whole unpleasant experience.

WANTED PREGNANCY

Genetic Counseling. If you're over 40 or have reasons to believe you might give birth to a physically or mentally deformed child, ask your obstetrician about amniocentesis. It's a procedure that can determine early in pregnancy (13th-16th week) whether an embryo will develop normally. It's saved many women from unnecessary abortion. Test available at these hospitals: Cook County, Michael Reese, Mount Sinai, Children's Memorial, and University of Chicago. Fees vary. Free at Cook County.

Fathers in Delivery Room & Rooming-in. Currently only four principal teaching hospitals allow a father in delivery room if mother and attending physician approve and if couple has had orientation (Lamaze course) prior to delivery. Hospitals are: Evanston, Michael Reese, Presbyterian-St. Luke's, University of Chicago. All but Presbyterian-St. Luke's also permit rooming-in of newborns. **For other hospitals in the Chicago area** that allow one or both, call Chicago Hospital Council, 751-0700.

Chicago Maternity Center, 1336 S. Newberry,† MO 6-3423. A Chicago institu-

---

* This is why you must not wait till the next day for an examination. Nobody's as likely to believe you if you've apparently been in no hurry to claim you've been raped.

† Will headquarter in Northwestern's Women's Hospital & Maternity Center when completed in 1975.

tion (a charity) that's been delivering babies at home since 1895. Delivers any woman in emergency, but hopes you'll register with it early in pregnancy. Primary obligation is to medically indigent despite growing middle-class interest in home delivery. Traveling delivery team of three consists of an obstetrical nurse, a Northwestern Memorial Hospital obstetrical resident, and a senior medical student. Northwestern Memorial Hospital used for patients who need hospitalization. Sliding scale fee; average payment for delivery $25, maximum fee $250.

PEDIATRICS

If you're a newcomer, find a pediatrician the same way you find any other physician—through one of the principal teaching hospitals below or those on p. 61-63. If you haven't a pediatrician, take a sick or injured child to an outpatient pediatric clinic at a teaching hospital or to one of these pediatric centers:

Children's Memorial Hospital, 2300 Children's Plaza, 649-4000. Major pediatric teaching hospital for Northwestern University medical school and official state-designated Children's Trauma Center. Takes children as new patients through age 16; previous patients to age 18. Has general and specialized clinics, including child guidance and development. Fees according to ability to pay. Emergency entrance on Lincoln Av. just north of Belden. Also:

> **Poison Control Center,** 649-4161. Advice by phone and immediate hospitalization when needed.
> **Trauma & Burn Units,** 649-4161
> **Psychiatric Emergency Care,** 649-4161

Kunstadter Children's Center of Michael Reese Hospital, 2915 S. Ellis. Has general and specialized clinics, mainly in Mandel Clinic building, 29th at Vernon. Fees according to ability to pay. Emergency room is in Mandel Clinic. Phone ahead for instant advice, 791-2840 from 8 AM-midnight; 791-2883 after midnight. Also:

> **Poison Control Center,** 791-2050
> **Psychiatric Emergency Care,** 791-2840
> **Pharmacy,** with prescription-filling service to midnight for prescriptions originally filled at the hospital, 791-2550
> **Dysfunctioning Child Center,** 791-4233. Extraordinary center for testing, diagnosis, and prognosis for young children whose problems have defied diagnosis and nobody knows what's wrong. Long waiting list—eight months or more. Fee according to ability to pay.

Wyler Children's Hospital, at University of Chicago, 5825 S. Maryland, 947-1000. Takes children through age 15. Pediatricians here are full-time faculty members, see children only at the hospital. Specialized clinics with set fees for the most part. Emergency entrance at Billings Hospital, 950 E. 59th. Also:

> **Poison Control Center,** 947-6231
> **Psychiatric Emergency Care,** 947-6231
> **Transfusion Component Service for Hemophiliacs,** 947-6231

Joseph P. Kennedy, Jr. Mental Retardation Research Center, 947-6206. Specializes in diagnosis, evaluation, and child care. Wide range of services. Fee adjusted to ability to pay.

Fantus Health Center of Cook County Hospital, 621 S. Winchester, 633-6610. Specialized free clinics ranging from Allergy to Well-Baby for children to age 17. One of the least-known teaching facilities in the city. By appointment only. Child sees the same physician at each visit.

Nicholas J. Pritzker Children's Hospital & Center, 800 E. 55th, 643-7300. A psychiatric hospital with outpatient services, including emergency care, short-term crisis therapy, and diagnostic testing. For children 2½ through 16. Fees based on ability to pay.

For other sources of child counseling and psychotherapy, see next section.

MENTAL HEALTH: COUNSELING & THERAPY

Institute for Psychoanalysis, 180 N. Michigan, 726-6300. Outstanding research and teaching center (psychiatrists come here for the five years of training necessary to become psychoanalysts). The Institute offers a number of services for adults and children (age 3 up): diagnosis; referral to psychiatrist or psychoanalyst for private consultation or treatment; referral to other psychiatric facilities that may be more appropriate; psychoanalytic treatment in its own low-fee clinic.

Wexler Clinic of Michael Reese Hospital, 2960 S. Lake Park, 791-3900, offers individual, family, group, and child therapy. Sliding scale fees: $1 to $24 per hour.

Illinois State Psychiatric Institute, 1601 W. Taylor, 341-8000. Though the state's open to criticism for its unwillingness to accept new patients—even psychotics—at its facilities, ISPI does see would-be patients within a week, less time if problem is urgent. Basically a training and research center (depression, schizophrenia), ISPI accepts inpatients on basis of its own research needs but in outpatient clinics gives help in far broader areas. Fees average $10-12 per visit.

Neuropsychiatric Institute of the University of Illinois Hospital, 912 S. Wood, 996-7362. Individual, group, and family therapy for children, students, adults. Special help for parents whose infants and toddlers show symptoms of psychiatric problems. Fee based on ability to pay.

North Shore Mental Health Assn., Irene Josselyn Clinic, 405 Central, Northfield, 446-8910. Superb community clinic serving the North Shore, though anyone can phone for evaluation. Staff includes psychiatrists, psychologists, child therapists, psychiatric and other social workers. Fee according to ability to pay.

Recovery, Inc., 116 S. Michigan, 263-2292. Self-help organization for former mental patients and nervous people who want to learn ways to handle the frustrations and irritations of everyday life. Techniques developed by a psychiatrist are taught by volunteers who have had Recovery training and are ex-patients themselves. Recovery groups meet throughout city and suburbs. For age 18 up. Yearly membership $7.50 for those who can afford; no fee for those who can't.

Thresholds, 1153 N. Dearborn, DE 7-7587. After October 1973, 2700 N. Lakeview, DE 7-7587. Warm professional help for discharged mental patients who want to get back into the mainstream. Individual counseling; job preparation; social, creative, and athletic activities. Walk in or phone first—it's up to you. Ages 16-50. Nominal fee adjusted to income.

SPECIAL TESTING & TREATMENT CENTERS

George & Anna Portes Cancer Prevention Center, 33 W. Huron, 944-4371. One of the few places in the country where a computer is always on your side. Modern nonprofit center offers multiphasic health screening. Tests include 100-mm chest X ray, hematology, urine, glucose, cholesterol, uric acid, electrocardiogram (EKG), blood pressure, vision, hearing. Specialists (MDs) complete examinations—physical, gynecological, proctoscopic. Results sent to your physician for his analysis and evaluation. Appointment essential. Fee $50; Xeroradiography (mammography) $20 extra.

Siegel Institute for Communicative Disorders, 3033 S. Cottage Grove, 791-2900. A Michael Reese Hospital & Medical Center facility for children and adults. Diagnosis and treatment of hearing and speech problems, special classes for hard-of-hearing children. Fee according to ability to pay.

Searle Communicative Disorders Center, 2299 Sheridan Rd., Evanston, 492-3128. This Northwestern University center offers help with learning disabilities, speech and hearing problems. For children and adults.

Both Siegel and Searle are new facilities specially constructed for what they do, superbly equipped, have excellent staffs.

Eye & Ear Infirmary of the University of Illinois Hospital, 1855 W. Taylor, 996-6500. Teaching center for all types of eye, ear, nose, and throat disorders. Houses the state eye bank; has one of the largest glaucoma clinics in the world, staff specialists for plastic surgery, laser-beam treatment. Most care given by graduate MDs taking their residency training, but staff specialists are available. New clinic patients registered Mon.-Fri. mornings, seen thereafter by appointment. Fees based on ability to pay.

Free glaucoma screening tests for anyone over 35 in a mobile unit maintained by **Illinois Society for the Prevention of Blindness,** WA 2-8710. Phone to learn when in your community. If examining MDs find signs of glaucoma or other eye diseases, they'll refer you immediately for follow-up to one of the big medical schools or hospitals that maintain eye clinics, or give you a list of qualified ophthalmologists.

Also free glaucoma screening clinics at Evanston Hospital every first and third Saturday and at Hinsdale Sanitarium & Hospital, in Hinsdale, every first Tuesday, Sept.-May 1.

Free chest X ray for TB detection at X-ray unit in City Hall and in clinics at 2849 N. Clark, 2160 W. Ogden, 3525 S. Michigan, 641 W. 63rd. For suburban locations, check your county TB Sanitarium District—for instance: Cook

County TB Sanitarium District, FO 6-5000; Lake County TB Sanatorium, 336-4010.

Illinois College of Podiatric Medicine, 1001 N. Dearborn, 664-3301. Walk-in clinic for care and treatment of feet by students in four-year course under supervision of doctors of podiatry. All outpatient surgery performed by graduate doctors of podiatry. Registration fee $7.50, $5 per visit.

Diabetes Testing. During National Diabetes Detection Week (third week in November), **Diabetes Assn. of Greater Chicago** gives free screening tests at approximately 60 hospitals in Chicago and suburbs. For nearest location, phone 943-8668. **Chicago Board of Health,** 744-3864, offers free tests year-round.

AGENCIES THAT HELP

Chicago is rich with agencies and service organizations that help anyone who is sick or handicapped. Here are the key organizations to call for information. If their staffs can't help directly, they know who can and will get you or your child to the right place.

Community Referral Service, Council for Community Services in Metropolitan Chicago, 64 E. Jackson, 427-9623. This is the biggest help-coordinating agency in the city. Its staff knows every source for any problem you can name: social, medical, physical, psychiatric, mental retardation; helps everyone who phones. For persons over 60, staff also maintains a special Information Center for the Aging, same phone as above.

For Alcoholism
   Chicago Council on Alcoholism, 6 N. Michigan, RA 6-1368. Start here if you've an alcoholic parent, spouse, employee, or are yourself an alcoholic who wants help. Free counseling and referral to whatever resources seem needed—Alcoholics Anonymous, Alanon, Alateen, Grant Hospital program for alcoholics, or Lutheran General Hospital (Park Ridge) alcoholism program. Mon.-Fri., 9 AM-5 PM, but appointments at other hours when necessary.

For Arthritis
   Arthritis Foundation, Illinois Chapter, 159 N. Dearborn, 782-1367. Services for anyone with arthritis include referral to one of 13 clinic centers the foundation supports and to physicians who specialize in arthritis. Clinic fee based on ability to pay.

For Birth Defects
   National Foundation March of Dimes, Chicago Chapter, 173 W. Madison, AN 3-1070. NF still helps those crippled by polio, but its major emphasis now is on birth defects. Offers counseling; referral; help with braces, crutches, other equipment. Also pays for outpatient physical therapy on MD's request.

For Blindness
   Agencies for the blind abound, and their programs vary widely. **Community Referral Service,** 427-9623, is your best bet for cutting through the maze—especially if you're trying to help a child, young adult, or adult become self-supporting and independent.

For Cancer
   American Cancer Society, Chicago Unit, 37 S. Wabash, 372-0471. Service department provides information, referral for home care, dressings, bandages, transportation; lends wheelchairs and sickroom equipment; has rehabilitation programs such as Reach for Recovery for mastectomy patients.

For Cerebral Palsy
   United Cerebral Palsy of Greater Chicago, 343 S. Dearborn, 922-2238. Central resource for the cerebral-palsied and their families. Referrals for medical help and to long-term-care facilities. Maintains special education center for children and young people (ages 3-21) not eligible for public school programs. Board of Education pays—you can sue Board if it doesn't. Also summer day camps for children. Adult services include counseling— psychological, sexual, vocational; year-round clubs; summer residential camps.

For Colostomy
   Colostomy Assn. of Chicago, 4734 W. Byron, 736-7189. Offers reassurance, companionship with other colostomates, practical advice, and monthly meetings with topical speakers.

For Cystic Fibrosis
   National Cystic Fibrosis Research Foundation, Northern Illinois Chapter, 63 E. Adams, 939-5166. Has centers at five teaching hospitals for complete testing and early diagnosis of CF and foots all the bills. Sends a staff nurse to home to help parents know what to expect and to help get equipment and drugs at reduced costs.

For Drug Abuse
   Illinois Drug Abuse Program (IDAP, p. 66) offers communities help with their drug abuse programs. Community Assistance Project shows you how to set up a program and get it operational.
   National Training Center on Drug Abuse, 5454 South Shore Dr., 324-1717, gives professionals and paraprofessionals free training in operation of drug treatment programs.

For Epilepsy
   National Epilepsy League, 116 S. Michigan, 332-6888. Many epileptics are unaware of the advantages of seeing a neurologist. League offers free referral service to these medical specialists and to clinics. Also maintains low-cost pharmacy for prescription drugs epileptics need.

For Handicaps, Physical & Mental
   Chicago Easter Seal Society, 220 S. State, 939-5115. *The* place to learn about available help and work programs for physically handicapped people. Among its services: therapy center for children,* equipment loans on MD certification, dental program exclusively for handicapped children. Booklet *Guide to Chicago Loop for the Handicapped* is a gem—25¢.

---

   * Includes speech therapy, occupational therapy, physical therapy, preschool play groups; takes children with communication disorders, cerebral palsy, spina bifida, cleft palate, mental retardation. Offers a type of therapy not available in schools. Has close parent contact, counseling, and home programs for children. By referral from MD, hospital, or other.

Co-Ordinating Council for Handicapped Children, 407 S. Dearborn, 939-3513. Help for parents of children and young people, infants up, who are physically or mentally handicapped. Here's where to learn what their rights are under Illinois law and how to get needed services from public and private organizations. Council provides fact sheets, booklets, a manual for group action; holds semimonthly parents' workshops.

Note: Illinois law provides public aid for individuals over 21 who have permanent physical or mental disabilities. The law states that such people are no longer the financial responsibility of their parents and therefore may receive public aid in their own right regardless of their parents' income. For additional information, phone State of Illinois Information Service, 793-2627.

For Hearing Impairment

Chicago Hearing Society, 30 W. Washington, 332-6850. Helps not just deaf or hard of hearing but teaches sign language to parents, co-workers, others who want to communicate with deaf. Low fee—$25—waived for parents and close family members who can't pay. Services to deaf include consultation; audiological testing; training in lipreading or use of hearing aids; parent counseling. Summer camp for ages 7-14; year-round social programs for teens, young adults, senior citizens. Nominal fee or no fee.

For Heart Disease

Chicago Heart Assn., 22 W. Madison, Fl 6-4675. Ask its Heart Information Service any questions about diseases of the cardiovascular system—heart attack, stroke, etc. Get referral to qualified cardiologists, rehabilitative help for patients, supportive help for families. Also referrals to sources of financial help for surgery, medication, equipment, home-care services. All services free.

For Kidney Disorders

Kidney Foundation of Illinois, 127 N. Dearborn, 263-2140. Referral to nearest nephrologist, a specialist in kidney diseases. Makes drugs available (MD referral needed) at considerable discounts—30-50%.

For Multiple Sclerosis

National Multiple Sclerosis Society, Chicago Chapter, 360 N. Michigan, 346-0783. Its Homebound program is a misnomer, for its wide variety of activities are designed to keep anyone with multiple sclerosis from being homebound: employment; social and community activities; field trips; classes in art, ceramics, sewing, choral singing, play reading, photography, swimming. Transportation available. No one turned away for lack of funds, but you pay if you can.

For Muscular Dystrophy

Muscular Dystrophy Assn. of America, 600 S. Michigan, 427-0551. Come here to learn if anything can be done that hasn't been done. Or to get diagnosis and orthopedic appliances (free on note from physician). Also, free summer camp for ages seven through adult; free clinics; parents' club.

For Sickle-Cell Disease

Midwest Assn. for Sickle Cell Anemia Research, 7936 S. Cottage Grove, 488-4700. If you suspect you might be a carrier or your child might have sickle-cell anemia, this is the place to start. Free referral to hospital centers for diagnosis, treatment, and counseling.

WORTH KNOWING ABOUT

Ambulances. A first-rate private ambulance service provides a clean ambulance, modern transport equipment, and well-trained personnel who have humanity. Neither the firm nor the drivers will demand payment before services are rendered. But, in this city, it's not illegal to refuse transport before payment, and you therefore could find yourself having a very rough time trying to rush someone to a hospital by private ambulance. If you don't believe this is a blood-and-guts business, look at the names listed under "Ambulances" in *Yellow Pages B*—every firm jockeying for head-of-column position by using oddball names compounded from the initial A.

On your own in a life-and-death situation where you want to get to a particular hospital* by private ambulance, ask the company you phone if it has EMT-A certified personnel and insist that's who they send. EMT-A (Emergency Medical Technician-Ambulance) is a national classification given ambulance personnel who've been through a rigorous three-month course. Training emphasizes emergency procedures, especially ways to stabilize whatever life forces exist.

Currently, some ambulance companies have personnel who've taken the full EMT-A course and passed it, but their ambulances may lack the necessary lifesaving equipment (oxygen alone may by no means be sufficient). Other companies may have the equipment, but their men may have taken only the Chicago Fire Dept. Emergency Course—a crash version of EMT-A. Furthermore, if all the ambulances in one company's fleet are out when you phone, the company will send an ambulance from another fleet with which it has reciprocal arrangements—and you have no idea what its standards are. Until the city forces the end of these discrepancies, no citizen has any guarantee that superior emergency private ambulance service is available when needed. Going rate in metropolitan Chicago is $40 plus $1 per mile from pickup to hospital, plus $6 for oxygen.

Chicago Fire Dept. has a fleet of 33 ambulances plus hospital-connected helicopters for emergencies like coronary, massive bleeding, traffic accident, etc. If you call because of gun or knife wounds or drug overdose or attempted suicide (it's against Illinois law to kill yourself), the police will come along to investigate.

Chicago Police Dept. has no ambulances, uses squadrols and squad cars in emergencies. By law, effective July, 1973, police and firemen take sick or injured persons to the nearest general hospital with an emergency room rated Comprehensive—and that's it.

Mobile Intensive Care Network. A two-way-radio-linked emergency ambulance pilot program for the state covering nine northwest suburbs: Arlington Heights, Palatine, Lake Zurich, Buffalo Grove, Hoffman Estates, Morton Grove, Mount Prospect, Rolling Meadows, Schaumburg.

Police, firemen, and some private ambulance drivers in these suburbs are clinically trained paramedics, able to handle life-and-death emergencies:

---

*In Chicago, only a private ambulance service delivers a person to the hospital of his choice.

coronary, poisoning, a child in convulsions, choking, trauma, etc. Their ambulances are equipped with portable cardiac defibrillators, electrocardiogram (EKG) hookups, drugs, intravenous, other lifesaving supplies. Their two-way radios keep them in constant contact with an emergency room physician at Northwest Community Hospital, Arlington Heights, and they follow his instructions for emergency care. The effort stabilizes a patient's condition so that he can be transported safely to the nearest hospital.

Jack's Livery Service, 4409 W. Washington, 379-4614. For people who must go to hospitals regularly for therapy or treatment, are too disabled to use cabs, but shouldn't pay for ambulances. Mr. Alfred Cain picks up at home, delivers gently to hospital, waits, makes return trip. Patients love the care they receive from this kind, elderly gentleman. Northwestern Memorial Hospital, the VA hospital on Huron, and Northwestern University medical school clinics all call on him constantly. In city, $14 per trip; higher to and from suburbs.

North Park Bus Co., 5149 N. Kedzie, dispatcher phone 935-2141. A Handibus service with hydraulic lifts. Picks up anyone who, because of disabilities, cannot use CTA; takes wherever one wants—to work, shopping, theatre, hospital, etc. Buses operate 6:30 AM-6 PM, may run evenings in near future. Call before 4 PM for next-day service. Minimum fee round trip $2.50. Owners trying to get federal funds so that service can be offered free.

All-Night or Nearly All-Night Pharmacies. Best not to get sick at night because nobody delivers prescriptions after 10 PM. Maybe a cab will pick up for you; otherwise, you fetch.

    Musket & Henriksen, 8401 N. Crawford, Skokie, OR 3-5940 (open all night seven nights per week); at 4200 N. Central, MU 5-2500 (to 2 AM).

    Northwestern Pharmacy, Inc., 1576 N. Milwaukee, HU 6-0987. Open all night seven days per week but never delivers.

    Schmid Drug, Inc., 6010 W. North, 889-8710. Open until 3 AM Mon.-Sat. (pharmacy closes at midnight), open to 10 PM Sun.

Drug Information Center for the state at University of Illinois Hospital, 996-6887, can answer questions about prescription drugs, their side effects, even identify foreign prescriptions. The service is intended for physicians and pharmacists but in an emergency will give you needed information.

Dept. of Health Education, American Medical Assn., 535 N. Dearborn, 751-6588. Answers general questions about the nature of illness, diseases, medications—for instance: "What is depression?" "What are the symptoms of appendicitis?" Physicians here cannot treat or diagnose by phone, but they will advise on, say, the kind of medical help you might need. Mon.-Fri., 8:30 AM-4:45 PM. Questions also answered by mail.

HMOs (Health Maintenance Organizations) are just coming into being in Chicago. Like Kaiser-Permanente groups in California and the Health Insurance Plan of New York City, HMOs here will be a form of prepaid admission to a group medical practice. A family joins through the breadwinner's place of employment, pays a fixed yearly fee (payable as a monthly premium), and the HMO guarantees to treat *all* the family's ills. Blue Cross will market as Co-Care (Coordinated Health Care) here.

Nurses. Normally, your physician finds a nurse for you. Otherwise, call **Illinois Nurses Assn.,** ST 2-8542. Remember, an RN (registered nurse) will not do anything but nurse.

Visiting Nurse Assn. of Chicago, 232 E. Ohio, 944-2585. Professional nursing care for any city resident who needs it. Nurses are RNs and LPNs (licensed practical nurses). Anyone can request evaluation visit. For continuing care, you must have written orders from your physician—VNA will help find an MD if necessary. Nurses make daily rounds (8:30 AM-4:30 PM), stay at each home long enough to give essential care but no longer. Adjustable fees; no patient refused because of inability to pay. Also will refer to VNA units in suburbs.

Alverna Home Nursing Center (Hospital Sisters of the Third Order of St. Francis), 1437 W. 51st, LA 3-3093. Theoretically, the remarkable Sisters here (all graduate RNs) confine their help to the aged who live in the area between 31st and 95th Sts., State St. west to Kedzie Av. Reality is something else. Sisters have taken terminal patients as young as 16, go beyond their boundaries when trips can be fitted to their schedules, try to find Sisters of other Orders to help when they can't. They're among the world's truly beautiful people, offering help on a wholly nonsectarian basis.

Homemaker services help families and individuals at time of crisis—a very ill mother or a mother's death, a single of any age suddenly bedridden—or anyone chronically ill.

North Suburban Homemaker Service, 518 Davis, Evanston, 864-6360, provides mature trained homemakers to North Shore suburbs Mon.-Fri., 9 AM-5 PM; helps find someone for weekends. Homemakers prepare meals, supervise children, do light housekeeping, provide personal health care under supervision of RN. A thoughtful social worker evaluates every request, provides counseling when needed to weather a crisis. Fee according to ability to pay—from zero to $140 per week.

Homemaker's Service, division of Child & Family Services, 234 S. Wabash, 427-8790, provides identical services throughout Chicago and suburbs.

Community Referral Service, 427-9623, helps you get to a community resource. Primarily for low income, but extenuating circumstances are always considered. Fee according to ability to pay.

Salvation Army has a homemaker service. Phone WH 4-0378, ask for intake secretary. Fee according to ability to pay.

Other Sources for Homemakers. American Registry for Nurses & Sitters (p. 96) and Merry Pop-in's (p. 95). Or phone the pastor, priest, or rabbi of a church or temple in your community—each man is likely to know of someone who can come in as a homemaker.

Nursing Homes. Very few good ones in the city; not many more in suburbs. Personal investigation is imperative—you cannot rely on brochures or phone interviews. Investigate during visiting hours so you can talk to people who are visiting. As models, use Whitehall Convalescent & Nursing Home or Balmoral Nursing Home in Chicago or Villa St. Cyril (a home for the aged, with nursing facilities) in Highland Park.

Try to get a nursing home with an MD on 24-hour call. Check his qualifications. If you have to settle for what's available or what you can afford, visit often and prevail on friends to visit too. A nursing home won't skimp on services or care if it knows someone concerned about a patient visits regularly.

If you have complaints, voice them—sometimes the people in charge don't know what their employees are doing. Check your bills—some get loaded with extras, but basically all you're paying for is bed and board. Wheelchairs, care of incontinents, special diets *are* extras.

Organ Donation. Call **Kidney Foundation of Illinois,** 263-2140, to learn how to donate desperately needed kidneys. Phone **Illinois Society for the Prevention of Blindness,** WA 2-8710, for card for eye donation after death.

Blood. Blood is an organ. It is living tissue. Under a new Illinois law, the use of blood from paid donors is prohibited except in extraordinary circumstances. The result is a continuous shortage. To make sure there's enough blood to go around—for you and everyone else—give blood. **Metropolitan Chicago Blood Council,** 332-2272 (24-hour phone), will name convenient locations for donating. Council also can advise on the blood-replacement plan that covers you and your family for as long as one year.

To leave your body to science for medical purposes, contact **Demonstrators Assn. of Illinois,** 2240 W. Fillmore, SE 3-5283. Its members are medical schools.

CHAPTER V

CLOUT & SAVVY

Every major American city operates on a system—ways of getting things done. New York's system is collapsing. Chicago's is tight and efficient. Chicagoans may bemoan the strength of machine politics in their city, but they don't vote Mayor Daley out of office—they reelect him. The feeling is: When Daley quits office, the machine will break down and so will the city.

The system here works to a great extent on a base of clout, fixes, deals, and trades. It's no different than elsewhere—only more obvious. Chicago is not a subtle city. The machine buys votes and judges. An astonishing number of Chicagoans brag about the number of times they've bribed cops. And everyone tries to get clout.

Clout is the Chicago term for influence based on obligation—the favor somebody owes you because you once did him a favor. At one end of the scale, it's a political favor; at the other, it's big tipping. Clout is assumed to be illegal—as in a traffic-ticket fix. But it may instead be ethically questionable—as in a multimillion-dollar land deal in which a slum owner, who is also a partner in a building syndicate, gets his slum property earmarked for urban renewal and then helps his business syndicate get the bid to develop the area for the Dept. of Urban Renewal. Clout can also mean more efficient ways of getting what you deserve from the city.

How do you get clout? By doing something helpful for somebody who has it. One way: become a registered voter; let your alderman and ward committeeman know you're alive. Use the small clout you can generate as an interested voter who backs them when you need help with legitimate problems, like building-code violations in your building, a youngster picked up on false arrest—this sort of thing.

Pitch into political campaigns. Volunteer time, contribute money, get involved—work. Read Mike Royko's *Boss* (Dutton, 1971); chapters II and III are a blueprint of the mundane beginnings that led Mayor Daley straight to clout and political power. Anybody who wants clout as much as Daley did can acquire it the way he did.

If your activity is devoted to the party with the most power in your ward, you can get what you want—but you ought to ask yourself what price you may eventually have to pay.

USING YOUR ALDERMAN

"A functioning alderman is an ombudsman for city affairs and a reliable guide to other government agencies."

LEON M. DESPRES, Alderman, 5th Ward

An alderman is expected to help with the following problems: personal safety, pollution, sanitation and noise complaints, malfunctioning city equipment or services (street lights out, garbage not removed, sewers stopped up or emitting foul odors), dirty restaurants in his ward, consumer gyps, wandering dogs, overzealous police, underzealous police, broken sidewalks and cracked curbs, abandoned buildings, neighborhood fire hazards, rodent control, landlord-tenant problems arising from building-code violations or inadequate heat, civil service exams, parking and traffic problems, dead tree removal, legal aid, problems in connection with immigration. You can direct some of these complaints to various city departments (p. 85-87). When results aren't forthcoming, you've the right to expect help from your alderman.

An alderman also ought to help with such neighborhood needs as a new school building and the creation of vest-pocket parks or playgrounds. And you hope he can give general information and advice. Whether he will do any or all of the above depends on the kind of alderman he is. Some machine aldermen do next to nothing for their constituents in terms of upgrading or even preserving the good elements of a neighborhood. Yet they get reelected through political naïveté or voter apathy or cash at election times or any combination of these.

Find your alderman through your ward committeeman's office; aldermen almost always share space with them. Republicans and Democrats have 50 ward offices each. To locate ward offices, call 744-3081. Independents have their own offices (p. 137), or call Board of Election Commissioners, DE 2-3050.

Cynical Chicagoans say you get better aldermanic services in a machine ward. True—if the alderman belongs to the handful of machine aldermen who have so much power they command instant action and fantastic expenditures in their wards. But a savvy Independent alderman has intelligent young people on his staff who know how to hound city departments for needed services. Furthermore, since the Independent can't rely on a machine power base to keep reelecting him, he works harder to understand the people in his ward and their problems.

To live in one of the countless wards where the alderman is a mediocre machine alderman may be the most dismaying possibility of all. The mediocrity is content to take care of ward necessities, but he lacks the imagination of the Independent and the power of the top machine alderman to upgrade his ward and make it a more desirable place to live.

As for ward committeemen: Alderman Despres says Chicagoans often think the ward committeeman is the person to see about illegitimate arrangements. In fact, a ward committeeman is a party official concerned primarily with patronage, selection of candidates, and getting out the vote. Still, if your ward committeeman is a Democrat, he can probably tell you whom to see and what to do to guarantee yourself a boat mooring in a Lake Michigan harbor. And a former social worker on a recent panel discussion said she got interested in politics in Chicago when she realized that the ward committeeman could get a youngster through Juvenile Court faster than any social worker could. A very powerful machine ward committeeman has clout, but if you go to him for a favor, best to ask yourself what the favor will cost.

NOT CLOUT BUT A LAWYER

Savvy is knowing a competent lawyer *before you need him.* In this city you should never buy a home, condominium, or cooperative or close any other real estate transaction by yourself. You want the most thoughtful lawyer you can find to go over the terms of the purchase.

Young couples, young people sharing apartments, women alone, and senior citizens especially ought to have a lawyer look at an offered apartment lease. The same people also ought not to buy a car, new or used, until a lawyer has looked at the contract.

Obviously, a lawyer is needed for divorces, adoptions, wills, lawsuits, youngsters in trouble with the police or the law. The question: How do you find a lawyer you can trust, and what's it going to cost? Big law firms charge $50 per hour or more for consultation and legal help. Free legal clinics* turn you down unless you can prove income below a certain level.

One good way to find the most able lawyer you can afford is to call a large law firm blind. Ask the switchboard operator to connect you with a lawyer. Chances are good that you'll be put in contact with a young idealist who probably spends his time working on corporate problems. His firm is big enough so that he can take ten minutes to talk to you and look for a referral for you. Remember to be explicit about what you can pay. Big law firms in Chicago include:

Kirkland, Ellis, Hodson, Chaffetz & Masters

Mayer, Brown & Platt

McDermott, Will & Emery

Isham, Lincoln & Beale

Sonnenschein, Levinson, Carlin, Nath & Rosenthal

Second best way to find a lawyer is through the lawyer referral plan of the **Chicago Bar Assn.,** 29 S. LaSalle, ST 2-7348. Lawyer conference hours 9-11:30 AM, 2-3:30 PM, Mon.-Fri. Conference fees $3 for half hour or less, $5 if more than half hour. The problem here is that names of available lawyers come up in rotation. You could get a good lawyer, but you could also get someone you won't be happy with.

Chicago Council of Lawyers, 53 W. Jackson, 427-0256. *The* place to turn if you've been a victim of police brutality, want to bring a civil damage action, need referral to a lawyer, or if you have complaints about a judge's conduct and can prove impropriety—rudeness or obvious bribe taking, for example. The council is a professional, reform-minded association of 1,200 lawyers affiliated with the American Bar Assn. Your case will be screened before referral.

ADAM (American Divorce Assn. for Men), 343 S. Dearborn, 922-4113, offers individual counseling, referral to lawyers who won't sell out, advice on being your own lawyer, etc. Organization is activist, intent on divorce reform and fairness for men. Worth investigating, especially if you want child custody or feel your wife's alimony claims are unconscionable. Reasonable fees. Spon-

---

* Legal Aid offices, Legal Aid Society of Chicago, 922-5625.

sors EVE for women with identical services. See also Divorce Anonymous, p. 134.

Mattachine Midwest, 4753 N. Broadway, 334-2244. A homosexual society that maintains a 24-hour answering service, calls on qualified members and professional aids to help with legal, psychiatric, and medical emergencies. See also p. 133.

CHICAGO POLICE DEPARTMENT

The CPD consists of approximately 13,000 of the highest-paid policemen in the country. They're well trained and tough. The toughness would be wholly admirable if it were used solely to deter violence and crime and apprehend criminals. But it is also used to "regulate" private morality—and if judged by their actions, most Chicago cops are apparently unable to differentiate between appropriate controls and unwarranted hassling of types they inevitably dislike. So they abuse kids with long hair and are ruthless with inoffensive homosexuals and harmless drunks and blacks and Latin Americans and the poor, who have no clout.

Unsophisticated or not, Chicago police will respond quickly to a call for help. In this respect, you can count on them. They're efficient, and if you're white, middle or upper class, and have been badly frightened, they can be kind.

District Police Stations. The city is divided into 21 police districts. A free folder, *Know Your Police District,* available from CPD headquarters, shows which district you live in, where the district office is and its phone, and gives some general information about the police. What the folder doesn't tell is why you should know the police in your district. This is why:

Knowing even one policeman at your district station is like having a friend in the neighborhood. It doesn't take much effort when you're outside to wave to the men who regularly patrol the neighborhood in a squad car, or to say hello. Or to ask a question or two about the neighborhood— "What's a good, cheap restaurant?" You'll get helpful answers, and you've broken the ice. Then you can ask the men in the squadrol to watch your home while you're out of town. You can call if there's trouble with a neighborhood youth—or a neighbor. If your dog is accused of biting but hasn't broken skin, a cop who knows the dog can calm an otherwise unpleasant situation.

If your adolescent is pulled into the district station and you're acquainted with a policeman there, you can more easily learn why and what to do about it. If your children get into trouble, a cop who knows them is more likely to act as a surrogate father than to haul them straight to the station. If you've been ticketed and don't know why, a cop who's a friend may take the time to get the facts for you.

Traffic Cops. For a number of reasons, the policeman who's exemplary when dealing with victims of crime becomes something else when a traffic cop. His daily ticket quota probably is more responsible than anything else. He has to make his quota even if that means writing marginal tickets, speed trapping, or resorting to subterfuge. Subterfuge includes lurking near a tricky intersection where a driver can all too easily make a wrong turn because of confusing signs or signal lights.* Or hiding near an intersection where left turns are prohibited between, say, 4 PM-7 PM and pouncing on a car that makes a turn at 6:59 PM when there's no traffic whatsoever.

The cop knows these actions are contemptible. He knows that lurk-and-pounce makes him look like a Keystone Kop. He also knows that because of stringent state license revocation laws, he's going to be offered innumerable bribes. He knows he's as tempted, as dollar-oriented, as cynical as anyone else. He knows that a traffic ticket given legitimately can be fixed—and that a strong case can be dismissed in court sometimes only because a judge knows the lawyer at the defendant's side. A policeman gets few chances for nobility as a traffic cop.

Shakedowns. Some cops are dollar-oriented, right? A traffic cop stops you, takes your license, and examines it. He's in no hurry to write a ticket, and he tells you repeatedly that he doesn't know what to do except give you a ticket. Some Chicagoans will say that the next move is up to you.

Bribery is common, but you have to make up your own mind. You may be more comfortable paying $15 in Traffic Court than $10 to the cop. Furthermore, bribery is a felony.

Newcomer's Tip. Chicago cops ticket excessively. You arrive here with a different set of standards, and you're in trouble immediately. To make it easier while you're learning about Chicago driving perils, use your out-of-state driver's license and license plates as long as legally possible, and if stopped, explain you're a newcomer to the city. The policeman will ask why you shot a light or whatever. Don't say why. Don't say anything. Just be polite. A policeman can't remember many, if any, of the people he stops. That's why, after he tickets someone, he sits in his squad car making notes on the back of the carbon copy of your ticket. Two months later he reads them over in court and acts like he remembers your case in explicit detail. This is called "refreshing one's recollection," but the refreshment needn't be at your expense. A traffic cop can't have much recollection if you haven't said anything.

TRAFFIC VIOLATIONS

Every Chicago cop carries a four-page folder of vehicle-code violations. When he needs to fish around for a way to nail you, he's got a minimum of 229 choices.

A free booklet, *Traffic Regulations: City of Chicago* (City Clerk's Office, Room 107, City Hall), contains the same information in a different but less lucid form. Still, everything you need to know is in it. With a specific question about violations or regulations, call the CPD, 744-4807.

How To Lose Your Driver's License. Under Illinois law, your license may be suspended or revoked if you're convicted of 3 *moving* violations within one

---

*If an intersection confuses drivers regularly and if the police are genuinely interested in reducing traffic accidents, then these signals should be reported and changed—not maintained as part of the city's revenue system.

12-month period. You'll certainly lose it if you're convicted on one of 30 major charges. See lists in *Illinois Rules of the Road*, free at any facility of Dept. of Motor Vehicles (p. 47) or any currency exchange that sells license plates.

Clout often plays a part in Traffic Court, and lawyers, city employees, friends of friends, and well-dressed, well-mannered adult whites have the best chance of getting the benefit of the doubt from judges. In court, continuances are called first, then the lawyers' cases, and then everyone else, generally in the sequence in which they presented themselves to the clerk on arrival. The clerk decides when cases are called. A defense that avoids the policeman's story is usually more successful than a head-on confrontation.

If it's the policeman's word against yours, the system demands his authority be upheld. With a lawyer at your side, your odds are better.

Note: Your Traffic Court date is set according to the policeman's rotating court appearance date so that he gets all his cases in a block. (Some judges will nudge their clerks to call all the cop's cases in succession, especially if the cop has been switched to night duty or is about to go on furlough.) If the cop happens to be on furlough during his court date, the city prosecutor might well call for a continuance—and get it. This is fair. You too can get a continuance the first time by arriving in court a little early and telling the clerk you want one. If a reason is given, it's usually that you need time to get a lawyer or must be out of town. If you're ill, send someone to request the continuance for you. Don't *not appear* only to come in later saying you were ill or out of town—that would create still more trouble for you.

Bail Bond. A cop who tickets you for a moving violation will ask if you want to surrender your driver's license or post a cash bond as security for your appearance in court. Sometimes the cop will let you substitute the bail bond card issued by your insurance company or automobile club. If you surrender your license, you're allowed to use the carbon copy of your traffic ticket as a driver's license within city limits. If you don't have an acceptable bail bond card (the police don't honor all of them) or if you need to keep your driver's license for out-of-city travel, go with the cop to the nearest police district station to pay a cash bond. Minimum deposit $25 *cash*. Personal checks not accepted. Cash bond mandatory if you're charged with a second offense after surrendering your driver's license.

Fines for lesser offenses, such as parking violations, can be paid in person at Traffic Court or by mail.

SAVVY: NOT BEING DEFEATED BY THE SYSTEM

Whom do you call when you've a complaint about a derelict city service? Who'll act in your behalf when you can't get title to a car you've just bought? Who can help you when you're the victim of fraud?

You have more resources at various governmental and private levels than you realize. That's what this section is about. If you need help with a bureaucratic problem not listed here and don't know what governmental agency has jurisdiction over it, call the Illinois Lieutenant Governor's office in Chicago, 793-2700; ask for the ombudsman.

Some government agencies have complaint departments per se. In dealing with those that don't, ask for the Public Information Officer, explain your problem, ask him to refer you to someone specific who can help.

Municipal Services

Heat, Insufficient. Mayor's Office of Inquiry & Information,* 744-3370. If line is busy, call Building Dept., 744-3420, and let the switchboard transfer your call. Also call your alderman. Chicago's heating ordinance covers the months between Sept. 15-June 1. Minimum allowable heat: 68° between 8:30 AM and 10:30 PM, a cruel 55° between 10:30 PM and 6:30 AM, 65° by 7:30 AM. The city says it sends representatives to verify complaints, and if conditions aren't corrected, city building inspectors will prepare court action. Maybe—but the process won't bring heat in a hurry except in a rare case the inspectors consider an emergency. It's almost faster to organize a tenants' union against a landlord who consistently fails to supply enough heat.

Garbage, Excessive. Mayor's Office of Inquiry & Information, 744-3370, or Dept. of Streets & Sanitation, 744-5000, or your alderman. If these sources fail to clean up littered alleys or stop a neighbor from maintaining rats on her garbage,† call Board of Health, 744-4000.

Dead Animal Removal (from street or alley), ST 2-5651

Sewers & City Catch Basins. For complaints about clogging, backup, foul odors, 744-7054. Emergency night and weekend phone, 744-3776.

Street Lights Out, 436-5475

Water Mains & Fire Hydrants, 434-8800

Parking Meters, Broken. Parking at a broken meter is illegal. If your coin jams a working meter and you're ticketed, phone Parking Meter Complaint Unit of Police Dept., 744-4815, so that meter can be checked immediately. Otherwise there's no way to prove whether the meter was broken at the time the ticket was issued. Duncan Parking Meter Maintenance Co. checks your complaint.

Abandoned Car Removal, 744-5513. If no action, phone your alderman.

Chicago Board of Health, Civic Center, 744-4000, defies understanding. In some situations it acts as a board of health should; in other instances, as in recent nursing home scandals, it shocks with its indifference to basic human welfare. An efficient board of health is both a protective agency and a watchdog for public health and concerns itself with everything from lead-based paint in old buildings to convalescent homes and unclean washrooms in public places. With a public health complaint, phone and hope for the best. If you write a letter of complaint, send it to Commissioner, Board of Health; state that you're sending a copy to the city desk of a newspaper or the news department of a radio or TV station. Then, send them.

Complaints & Claims Against the City. More people have legitimate complaints against the city than they realize. Example: It's night, you're driving

---

* This office says it also handles complaints about paint, plaster, defective wiring and plumbing, stray dogs, tree removal and trimming, broken curbs, police department.

† If you're a woman with a complaint about rats in garbage, on neighborhood streets, or in parks, do not bother phoning the city's Dept. of Rodent Control. The men who answer the phones are convinced women cannot differentiate rats from squirrels. To get action from Rodent Control, ask a man to phone in your complaint as his complaint.

along a dark street, you crunch into a chuckhole that has neither warning sign nor barricade. Your car frame is bent, your axle damaged. The city is clearly derelict in maintaining the street properly.

Write to the alderman of the ward in which this accident occurred. State the facts, state that you consider the city responsible and feel you deserve restitution for damages. Send copies to your own alderman and to the proper city department, in this case Streets & Sanitation. One or both aldermen should tell you to file a claim in the City Clerk's office (there's a form for complaints against the city). The form, along with your copies of estimates for repairs or receipts for bills paid, will be submitted to the Finance Committee in City Council. When Finance approves your claim, the matter will come up in City Council as a matter of routine. Within three-six months you'll get a check.

Utilities

Deficient Service or Improper Billing. Start with the consumer service department maintained by each utility—telephone, electric, or gas company. If nonproductive, turn to "Using Press Clout" (p. 89) or to the Illinois Commerce Commission, 160 N. LaSalle, 793-2850. ICC regulates rates of all Illinois utilities and has clout.

Transportation

Moving Complaints (against van line). When you can't get settlement of a claim for damaged goods or when you believe the van line charges are unfair, write to Director, Illinois Commerce Commission, 160 N. LaSalle, 793-2850—if your move was within the state. Write to Regional Director, Interstate Commerce Commission, 219 S. Dearborn, 353-6185, if your move was transcontinental or at least across state lines.

Automobile. For problems of licensing, title clearance, wresting a title from a dealer, car registration or theft, call Investigating Officer, Illinois Dept. of Motor Vehicles at any of its offices (p. 47). If the condition of a used car you bought was grossly misrepresented, phone Consumer Fraud Bureau, Illinois Attorney General's office.

Passenger Train Service. For complaints about intercity service, when you can't get satisfaction from the railroad or Amtrak (the National Railroad Passenger Corporation), write to the Interstate Commerce Commission. Direct Amtrak complaints to Manager, Customer Service, Amtrak, 955 L'Enfant Plaza North, SW, Washington, D.C. 20024. Commuter service and fares are regulated by the Illinois Commerce Commission.

Airlines. For complaints about fares, baggage, poor service, compensations for actions such as overselling your flight and bumping you for a long layover,* write Director, Consumer Affairs, Civil Aeronautics Board, 1825 Connecticut Av. NW, Washington, D.C. 20009.

---

* A long layover is more than two hours after scheduled departure on domestic flights, more than four hours on foreign flights. "Passengers eligible for denied boarding compensation, shall be compensated at the rate of 100% of the value of the first remaining flight coupon on their tickets with a $200 maximum and a $25 minimum." Assuming you were eligible for flight (not mentally deranged or too drunk to fly), airline should give you this information printed on a Notice Compensation for Denied Boarding slip. Downgrading from first class seating to coach is not considered denied boarding.

Insurance. For problems with auto, life, accident, and health insurance, such as settlement of claims, unjust cancellations, premium financing, contact Illinois Dept. of Insurance, Complaint Division, 160 N. LaSalle, 793-2433.

Consumer Fraud. Five government units handle complaints of fraud, false pretense, false advertising, deceptive practices connected with cash or credit sales.

Consumer Sales, Weights & Measures, City Hall, 744-4092. Here's a tough city department to handle complaints about retailers and firms or individuals promising services to be rendered within city limits but not fulfilling the promises. Handles misrepresentation, short weights and short measures, misrepresented warranties, bait and switch (advertising nonexistent or short-supply merchandise with attempt to get you to accept a substitute). Short measure includes draperies and carpets that don't fit because they aren't what you ordered. Also get help here on prepaid or partially paid furniture, ordered through a Chicago retailer but manufactured out of state, that apparently never will arrive despite a promise of delivery in 30-60 days.

Fraud & Consumer Complaints Division, Cook County State's Attorney's Office, Civic Center, 443-8425. Investigates crimes of a financial nature, generally but not always arising from contracts. For instance: deception in car purchase (like failure to transfer title); bush (charging customer more on written contract than was agreed upon orally); real estate transactions, such as failure to remit earnest money; transactions involving personal property; bad checks; forgeries; theft by deception; license violations; bigamy. Phone to see if your case is one the department handles—then request consultation with a staff lawyer. If crime is involved in your case, a hearing will be called. If not, you'll be referred elsewhere.

Consumer Fraud Bureau, Illinois Attorney General's Office, 134 N. LaSalle, 793-3580. Holds informal hearings, can subpoena and can go to court and put a firm out of business. Hence, is a highly effective agency because it can call in crooked dealers and scare the hell out of them. The state's Consumer Fraud Act, Retail Installment Sales Act, and Motor Vehicle Retail Installment Sales Act are almost incomprehensible to anyone but a lawyer (copies available in this office), but they are strong acts, and they do protect consumers. Come here with complaints involving deception of any kind, misrepresentation of goods (show proof of purchase), omission of essential information, unconscionable transactions.

Note: Legal Aid offices also handle consumer complaints. To locate a neighborhood office for someone who qualifies for its help, call Legal Aid Society of Chicago, 64 E. Jackson, 922-5625.

Federal Trade Commission, 219 S. Dearborn, 353-4423. Investigates complaints arising from interstate commerce only, such as mail fraud, bait and switch, false claims, product safety.

Food & Drug Administration, District Office, 433 W. Van Buren, 353-7379. Investigates complaints concerning purity, potency, safety, and labeling of foods, drugs, cosmetics shipped interstate; also toys and hazardous household chemicals shipped interstate. Will want to know where you purchased a product, whether an injury was involved (and if so, where your physician can be reached)—this sort of thing. Cannot use your sample of a bug in a can of food in court but will start investigation on basis of such a complaint.

Job Discrimination. Illinois Fair Employment Practices Commission, 189 W. Madison, 793-2240. On the federal level, go to **Equal Employment Opportunity Division** of Commerce Dept., 32 W. Randolph, 353-7625.

Environment. Your problem here may well be one of too many resources rather than too few:

> **Chicago Dept. of Environmental Control,** 320 N. Clark, 744-4080
>
> **Cook County Dept. of Environmental Control,** Civic Center, 443-7655
>
> **Illinois Environmental Protection Agency,** Naval Armory, Randolph at lakefront. Air pollution, 341-4696; water pollution, 793-3730; noise pollution (Springfield), 217-525-3334
>
> **Citizens Against Noise,** 2729 W. Lunt, 274-0980. An action group that's effective in publicizing the need for noise control.

Pro Se (Small Claims) Court, Civic Center, Room 602, Randolph at Dearborn, 443-8100.

A do-it-yourself court for cases involving any claim of $300 or less— like small claims involving auto accidents, warranties, return of security deposits. File your complaint and summons forms here with the help of senior law students. Filing costs, $9.50. Your case will come to trial in about six weeks. The beauty of this new court is that you can easily handle your own case when it comes up for trial; bring witnesses if you need them. The presiding judge knows you're unfamiliar with legal jargon and court procedure—is understanding and helpful, especially if you're up against a defense attorney.

Using Press Clout. Four Chicago newspapers offer column help with consumer complaints, requests for information, and cries for help in the entire range of human needs (including dire). In the *Daily News* it's "Beeline," in the *Sun-Times,* "Help-Mate." The *Trib* has "Action Express." *Chicago Today* runs "Action Line," and it can be terrific. For two examples of these columns at their best, see the "Action Line" quote (p. 91) and the "Beeline" quote (p. 91-92). Alas, the *Trib* is never as forthright. One caution here: your letter may not be answered. Staffs aren't large enough to handle the volume of mail, though each paper tries to speed urgent requests for help in the area of human problems.

Action Organizations. Two local organizations are committed to the improvement of life and government in Chicago. Neither can help you solve individual problems, but they'll listen to complaints and take action on a broad scale if warranted.

Businessmen for the Public Interest, 109 N. Dearborn, 641-5570. BPI is an investigative, not-for-profit organization chartered in 1969 to help solve major urban and environmental woes of the kind that affect everyone in Chicago—poverty, deterioration of communities, parks, Lake Michigan, prejudice and discrimination, human and civil rights, conflict of interest in local government. Operates somewhat like Nader's Raiders but takes injustices to court. A complaint about a smoking chimney doesn't belong here. A complaint about cop shakedown of minority group shopkeepers does. Reports of each year's effort available on request. Track record to date is good.

Better Government Assn., 75 E. Wacker, 641-1181. BGA investigates local government at all levels and is recognized as the best organization of its kind in the country. Much of its strength comes from fact that it won't take contributions that will obligate it. BGA accomplishes a great deal with a relatively small staff, was the major investigating group on recent vote fraud, ambulance, and nursing home scandals. (The last two are in its area of interest because ambulances and nursing homes are licensed by the state.) Phone if you have evidence of payoff, bribe taking, or other forms of corruption.

MACAP (Major Appliance Consumer Action Panel), 20 N. Wacker, 236-3165. When you can't get anywhere with the manufacturer of a faulty major appliance (washer, dryer, refrigerator, etc.), complain here to get action. Outside of city, call collect if necessary.

If you feel like taking a swat at a large corporation and think Ralph Nader could be interested, write him care of Consumer Reports, P.O. Box 1000, Mount Vernon, New York 10550.

FIXES & BRIBES

All bureaucracies breed corruption. In Chicago, bribery and payoff are common—and sometimes unavoidable. For instance, building inspectors can make your life miserable and even prevent you from remodeling your own home until you show appreciation in a specific way. Conversely, one reason so many new apartment high rises are in violation of the city's building code is that a building inspector was paid handsomely to overlook certain construction shortcuts. Two other examples:

At the Dept. of Motor Vehicles offices on a day when the inspectors feel impoverished, the going rate to pass the driving part of the license test is at least $10. One 76-year-old lady beat the racket this way: When the inspector told her for the third time that his name was Joe ————, she said smartly, "Well, Joe, you've done a very nice job," and sat back, her hands folded quietly in her lap. He passed her.

If you fail the test twice and are not interested in bribery, go to a driving school for a refresher course; the schools have got to have a way of assuring students they will pass. If you ask an inspector which school to attend, figure the one he recommends pays him a kickback for sending you— thus, the circularity of corruption.

There's a black market in Lake Michigan boat moorings, and you can't do a thing about it if you want a mooring—except pay. Should you decide to expose the payoff afterward, get your boat out of the lake first—so it's not wrecked in an "accident."

CAVEAT EMPTOR

1. Don't take complaints about cops to Police Internal Affairs Division.* IAD was created in 1960 to investigate charges of police misconduct. But as it now functions, the best description of IAD is: a turnaround. You may have a legitimate charge against a policeman, but unless he's already in

---

* Take them to Chicago Council of Lawyers (p. 82).

trouble with the department (and the department has been waiting for one final accusation), your complaint will be used against *you*. For instance, if among other things, the offending policeman arrested you, IAD will try very hard to make sure you're convicted. If you have both a good defense against the charge in the arrest and a good complaint against the policeman, IAD will do its best to see that you, not the cop, are discredited, and you are likely to wind up signing a release against any prosecution of the cop. So much for your citizen's complaint. This situation may change; 1973 began with a new state's attorney who can change it.

2. Beware of a tow pirate named Ross Cascio and his Lincoln Towing Service. Do not even consider parking in any supermarket lot after hours or in somebody's space behind an apartment building if a sign shows that the lot is protected by Lincoln Towing and that your car will be towed away at your expense. Cascio runs a 24-hour business with radio dispatched tow trucks. You can be in personal danger if you attempt to protect your car from one of his crews. No city ordinance exists at this time to govern the towing business, so Cascio can also charge anything he wishes before he gives your car back—$30 cash is the current rate. The following advice from "Action Line," *Chicago Today* (Nov. 20, 1972), makes sense:

> "My car was towed from 2926 N. Hampton Ct. by Lincoln Towing, 1301 W. Fullerton Av., Oct. 29. I paid them their $30. After getting home, I found the car wouldn't go into park. I also found the right side of the car is smashed in. All the towing company would say is: 'Tough, get a lawyer.' "—Lester Abraham

> ACTION LINE: Of course, Lincoln Towing isn't going to co-operate with Action Line. The firm has built its business on bad publicity. Even lawsuits ultimately seem to rebound to their benefit. We suggest you and others harassed by this towing firm follow its advice. Get a lawyer. Instead of suing Lincoln, however, make it the owner of the property from which your car was towed away. Such parties will not have the same stomach for lawsuits. Furthermore, they might just learn that smearing a large sticker on the driver's window is just as effective at keeping parking lots empty at night and—by avoiding legal fees—a lot cheaper.

3. An auction of abandoned autos held at a city auto pound is no place to buy a car. The following quote from "Beeline," *Chicago Daily News* (Aug. 13, 1971), shows why:

> At an auction of abandoned cars held at a city auto pound and run for the city by a professional auctioneer, I bought what the auctioneer presented as a 1970 Volkswagen, for $495. My bill of sale also said 1970. But later I learned—and had verified by the Nelson-McGann Volkswagen agency—that the car is a 1968 model. I feel that either the auction firm or the city should give me a price adjustment, but neither will. The auction firm said that it presented the car just as the police represented it to the firm. The City Council Finance Committee, to which I then made a claim, disallowed the claim. How is this for sharp dealing?—G. C., Chicago

The city, it turns out, is one of the most hard-nosed horse traders we have come up against yet; we hate to say it, but we couldn't move it any more than you could. The Finance Committee (whose action was approved by the full council) formally puts it this way: "This is a claim for the courts to decide. The city is not liable for the purchase of a car at public auction; when one bids on a car, he takes what he bids on." Both the city and the auction firm said you had a chance to look at the car before you bought it; but, of course, as Volkswagen itself says, its models don't look much—if any— different from year to year. We can't blame you for accepting what the auctioneer said. But, while we had no luck in our efforts for you, we wonder if your experience might not make people ask themselves whether they Would Want to Buy a Used Car from This City. What's that Latin motto on the city seal? Caveat emptor?

4. You can't buy fresh meat after 6 PM in any supermarket or butcher shop because the meatcutters' union has a stranglehold on its meat department. Get around that stupidity by cultivating the owners of a small independent store that sells fresh meat.

5. Illinois does *not* have a law requiring embalmment before burial,* but most funeral directors will try to persuade you such a law exists. Illinois does not have a law specifying that a casket be placed in a cement vault or grave box, but most cemeteries make their own "law" about this. If you're shopping ahead for cemeteries, check.

Funeral costs are mainly determined by casket price—$3,000 average if you get hung up on an unnecessary metal casket. Greedy funeral directors will always try to sell you the most expensive casket in the house. Alternatives to wholly unconscionable funeral costs are:

A. Insist on immediate burial—24 hours or less in a wood and cloth-covered casket. Do not use a funeral home for a wake, for viewing, or for a service. Have a memorial service after burial in a church, temple, or your home. Specify this in your own will if you wish.

B. Join **Chicago Memorial Assn.,** 59 E. Van Buren, 939-0678. It's a non-profit cooperative that believes the dignity of a funeral or memorial service is based on simplicity. CMA helps members select a funeral director in agreement with its goals and get all needed services for far less than the $1,100-4,000 that is the current rate for funerals and burials in Chicago. Through CMA, a funeral with burial is about $500.

C. Donate you body to medical science (p. 79).

---

* Except in deaths from smallpox, bubonic plague, or cholera or if the body is to be shipped interstate.

CHAPTER VI

PRACTICAL MATTERS

MONEY

To Establish Credit. If you've good credentials from wherever you've come plus a job lined up in this city, getting credit is easy. Go to a bank and open a checking account (usually $200 minimum for a regular account*). Next, fill out an application at the bank for a Master Charge card or BankAmericard. Then go to Marshall Field & Co., 111 N. State, and apply for a charge account. From here on, you'll have no trouble opening other charge accounts. A Field's charge is excellent identification and can be used as such in lieu of a driver's license.

If you're young and have never had charge accounts and your first credit applications are refused, go in person to credit managers. Face-to-face interviews can make a difference. Bring along any proof of payment of sizable cash purchases, say $550 paid for new furniture or $800 for a used car. These are good references you can't show on a standard credit application.

To Get Instant Cash. You cannot pop in at a branch bank to cash a check because Illinois does not permit branch banking. Apply for a credit card at a major hotel like the Drake or Conrad Hilton. These hotels will cash checks against their credit cards on a 24-hour basis. Don't bother with the Ambassadors East and West. Unless you frequent them so regularly you're considered a prize patron, you'll be limited to $25 or $30 per check.

Marshall Field & Co. courteously cashes your personal check—up to $100 —against its charge plate; not many other stores do.

LaSalle National Bank, 120 W. Adams, has a 24-hour money vending machine in its arcade. With a LaSalle checking account and a special card, you can cash up to $100 every 24 hours.

First National Bank, One First National Plaza, vends money through machines in outer lobby (Dearborn & Madison) on similar basis. Get up to $150 every 24 hours with a special card (FIRST/24) that represents your savings or checking account at First or your BankAmericard or any combination of these.

Supermarkets—major chains especially—cash checks once you're officially registered. Most limit personal checks to a maximum of $50.

Currency Exchanges—robbers all. Their state license is merely a license to operate. Incredibly, the state allows each CE to set its own rates. The smaller your check, the greater the rate percentage, 35¢ on a $10 check but only 60-75¢ on $100. Register in advance if you plan to cash checks.

Foreign Currency Exchanges. Loop banks like Harris Trust & Savings, Northern Trust, Continental Illinois, and First National buy and sell foreign

---

* Maximum monthly service charge if your balance falls below $200 is only $2.

currency. Continental Illinois also has a facility for this purpose at O'Hare Airport.

S/Ls. Illinois allows Savings & Loan Associations. They're similar to banks in that they carry savings accounts (they pay ¼% more interest than banks). Unlike full-service banks, S/Ls do not offer checking accounts and make personal loans only against whatever amount you have in your savings account. They are, however, excellent places to shop for mortgage loans on homes and condominiums.

CREDIT PROBLEMS

If you're unfairly refused credit because of a bad report from a credit-reporting agency, the Federal Fair Credit Reporting Act allows you to get the name and address of the agency. The agency must tell you the "nature and substance of all information" in its file on you. The **Credit Information Corp. of Chicago,** 425 N. Michigan, 645-5811, checks credit of Cook County residents and should give you an interview after you've filled out an application.

When a computer error is ruining your credit and you can't correct the error through normal channels, get the name of the president of the store or organization and write to him. Apologize for dumping your problem in his lap, state the problem, then say there's apparently no other way to get the mess straightened out except through him. Writing to presidents is remarkably effective.

Personal Finance Mess? Bail out one of these ways:

First National Bank, One First National Plaza, 732-4000. Go to its Plan-Ahead Center for free, comprehensive financial advice from young counselors. You don't have to bank at the First to use this service, and you won't be pressured to bank there.

Family Financial Counseling Service, 192 N. Clark, 641-6750. Services range from straightforward budget counseling (free) to a debt-management program that takes over your paychecks and pays your creditors at a predetermined rate (maximum fee to you $2.50 weekly). FFCS is supported by the business community.

Note: If you're earning upward of $12,500 yearly and can't make ends meet, ask an officer at your bank for referral to a financial counselor. If your income is modest and you're in a bind because of bills, try writing a letter to each creditor saying you know you owe X dollars, you can't pay it as fast as it should be paid, but you'll pay $2 (or whatever) per week plus usual interest and not charge or buy any more on credit until the bill is paid in full. This kind of letter plus weekly payments demonstrates your good intentions.

HOUSEHOLD HELP

Cleaning Lady. Current in-town rate for a cleaning lady is $15-17 (includes carfare). Going rate on the North Shore is $20-23.

Best way to find a cleaning lady is through the one who works for a ·

friend. Next best way is through the doorman in a high rise. Tip doorman generously. Another way, place ads in Chicago dailies and in foreign language newspapers. Check "Situations Wanted" in neighborhood papers. In suburbia, advertise in the local paper covering the widest area. Also, check supermarket bulletin boards in your neighborhood and in every high-rise laundry room you can get into.

Live-in Help. Run ads in Chicago dailies and foreign language press. Check "Maid Service" and "Employment Agencies" in *Yellow Pages B*. Checking the latter category is a big nuisance because R. H. Donnelley doesn't break down employment agencies by categories, but maid service agencies are there.

For very classy household help, including child nurses, chauffeurs, butlers, personal maids, cooks, second girls, gardeners, etc., call **Jane Estabrooks Household Registry,** 47 E. Oak, DE 7-6142.

Bonded Cleaning Services. If you live in a high rise or suburban development, ask the management office which firm it recommends. Hire the kind of cleaning help you need by the hour (usually a four-hour minimum) or by the day. A friendly service will try to book someone you like on a regular basis. If you want her full time, you eventually try to lure her away. **Merry Pop-in's,** a division of Manpower, Inc., 1360 N. Lake Shore Dr., DE 7-7900, offers the widest range of bonded household services along with party services, nursing and companion services, vacation services, dog walkers, and window washers.

Student Help. Call Student Placement or Director of Admissions at colleges, universities, or the Art Institute for part-time workers or live-in students who'll assume chores, including baby-sitting, in return for room and board. Or place an ad in a student newspaper. Male students often do yard work and heavy duty cleaning. Pay is about $2.15 to $3 per hour.

University of Chicago, 753-1234

Mundelein College, 262-8100

Northwestern University, Chicago Graduate Schools, 649-8416; Evanston Campus, 492-3291

Loyola University, North Sheridan Road Campus, BR 4-3000; Lewis Towers Campus, WH 4-0800; no baby-sitting per se

DePaul University, Lewis Center (Loop), WE 9-3535; Mid North Campus, LI 9-6900; no baby-sitting per se

Roosevelt University, 341-3500; big on baby-sitting

Columbia College, 467-0300

University of Illinois Circle Campus, 996-3130; commuter campus—big on live-in jobs

Illinois Institute of Technology, CA 5-9600; no baby-sitting per se

City Colleges of Chicago. Look in *Chicago A* for college nearest you.

Counselors from **Bucky's Boys Club,** 2275 Telegraph, Deerfield, WI 5-0691 or WI 5-3575, look for yard work on the North Shore.

BABY-SITTERS

All registries are top-heavy with older women but will honor requests for a woman under 30-40 if one is available or for a specific sitter who turns out to be one of your child's favorites. With young, active children ages six months to seven years, insist you don't want a frail old lady.

Chicago Parents Club, 5347 N. Clark, UP 8-4270. Mrs. Abbate investigates all sitters—good young grandmother types ages 40-55, students and business girls age 20 up. CPC is bonded and licensed. Membership fee of $10 covers the cost of finding sitters for you 12 times. Sitters get hourly fee of $1 up depending on number of children in family, etc. Four-hour minimum plus bus fare refund.

Lull A Bye, 6339 N. Minnehaha, RO 3-2282. Good, conscientious sitters and homemakers who'll come in while you're gone for the weekend. Homemakers go as far as 150 miles from Chicago; sitters serve all Chicago and suburbs.

American Registry for Nurses & Sitters, 3921 N. Lincoln, 248-8100. Baby nurses, licensed practical nurses, unlicensed practical nurses, homemakers for city and suburbs. Also baby-sitters but area limited to North Side.

Other Good Sources for Sitters: Retirement and church- or synagogue-sponsored old people's homes. Example: Mather Home, Evanston—filled with retired business and professional women. Those who want to be sitters are splendid—a lady who managed the children's book department at Field's, a kind grandmotherly lady who sits to finance a bird-watching trip to Mexico.

Call women's residences like Three Arts Club WH 4-6250, Eleanor Assn. 236-5589, Dearborn Club DE 7-9203, Lincoln Park Girls Club LI 9-8670.

Student Nurses. Some hospitals help their student nurses find babysitting work; others won't assume the responsibility. Phone those in your area, ask to be connected with whoever handles student nurse jobs. You may be investigated before any student nurse is permitted to sit for you. Current rate about $1.25 per hour plus transportation.

If you live in or near a high rise, ask the doorman for names of resident sitters, usually tenants' teen-age daughters or single women.

Call nearest high school. Ask to speak to the job counselor.

DRY CLEANING & LAUNDRY

Dry cleaners listed here are Chicago's finest and operate their own plants. Expect most of them to charge more than the corner cleaner who operates on a cash-and-carry basis.

Davies, 2349 S. Cottage Grove, CA 5-4204. Sends everything back stuffed with blue tissue paper. Will do the whole house too—rugs, furniture, draperies. Laundry service is so expensive (five-lb. bundle $3.75; each additional lb. 37¢) most people use only for very special things.

Marshall Field & Co., 111 N. State, ST 1-1000 or Customer Service ST 1-1050. Dry cleaning department on 7th floor especially good for laces and precious materials. Also furs, leathers, suedes, draperies. Will pick up and deliver. Service desks in suburban branches.

French Hand Laundry, 1701 N. Milwaukee, 772-2700. Not French and not a hand laundry but a fine laundry nevertheless. Ask for Bellview Service if you want hand pressing (shirts 80¢ each, fine tablecloths $2.25 and up per yard).

On regular laundry, six-lb. bundle $3.08; each additional lb. 25¢. Also dry cleaning, including draperies, rugs, leathers, suedes; reweaving and repairs. Cash/carry outlet, 2214 N. Clark, LI 9-7512. Dry cleaning prices 10% lower.

Poppy Cleaners, 4014 N. Broadway, BI 8-5000. Here's the kind of cleaner you want on a week-in-week-out basis. Excellent cleaning and reasonable—dresses $1.90 up; winter coats $2.35 up; men's suits $1.90 up.

Schultz Dry Cleaners, 1152 Central, Wilmette, AL 1-2775. Ends the complaint that there are no good, reasonably priced cleaners on the North Shore. Dresses and men's suits $1.95; lined dresses $2.50.

North Chicago Laundry, 2901 N. Clybourn, BI 8-3210; Skokie area 679-3971; North Shore suburbs 432-4551. Low loss ratio. If you're very fussy, regular machine-ironed flatwork may occasionally leave you wishing you'd done it yourself. Six-lb. bundle $3.19; each additional lb. 24¢. Ask for VIP service and pay more—$1 per yard for a tablecloth, for instance.

Leslie Koves, 17 N. State, AN 3-6829. Small specialty shop does a fine job of cleaning and repairing suedes and leathers on a cash-and-carry basis. Also reweaving, hemstitching, buttonholes and belts made to order, handbag repair and mounting needlepoint.

Charles A. Stevens, 25 N. State, RA 6-1500. Beautiful cleaning of furs, leathers, suedes in fur salon, 6th floor.

DRAPERIES

Services include pickup, delivery, and rehanging.

Hamen's Custom Interior Cleaners, 1257 W. Loyola, HO 5-4000. When you've put a small fortune into draperies, this is the firm to call.

American Drapemasters, 7513 W. Irving Park, 625-2070. Very good work at fairly reasonable prices. Also remakes draperies to fit new windows if you move.

RUGS, WALL-TO-WALL CARPETING, UPHOLSTERED FURNITURE

Wade Wenger Servicemaster, 320 S. Franklin, WE 9-0808. The firm's reputation was built on excellent wall-to-wall carpet cleaning. Now also does floors, furniture, and walls.

Imperial Carpet & Furniture Cleaners, 1737 W. Howard, RO 1-0041. Very good on upholstered pieces. Also does furniture touch-up.

Richards Custom Carpet & Furniture Cleaner, 236 Valley View Dr., Wilmette, HO 5-3200 or AL 1-2707. Reliable North Shore firm makes Chicago house calls too. Also sells and dyes carpets.

Associated Rug & Furniture Cleaners, 3017 W. Fargo, SH 3-8744. Jolly Mr. Maurice Weisman is the man to call for worn carpets that must take still more child and pet abuse. Remodeling available. Relaying taken for granted.

Wilson Rug Cleaners, 4240 N. Pulaski, 286-3477. Fair prices from accommodating people who do nice work. Specialize in blocking and cleaning needlepoint rugs. Services limited to Near North and North Shore. Will pick up and relay.

Ashjian Sourian (Ashjian Bros.), 1216 E. 47th, 538-3000. Good wall-to-wall rug and carpet cleaning and repair.

Nahigian Bros., 737 N. Michigan, 943-8300. Has its own spray process to eliminate brush friction and uses it on all rugs. Also repairs and restores.

Boyajian, 2247 N. Lincoln, DI 8-5469. Cleans and repairs but doesn't restore.

TAILORS

The neighborhood tailor isn't entirely a man of the past, and if he's middle-aged, he's probably a true craftsman. Otherwise try:

Playboy Bldg. Tailor Shop, 919 N. Michigan, MO 4-0055. Sam Kail's alterations on men's and women's clothes are expensive but excellent. He'll also send out shoes for repair and clothes for dry cleaning.

Park Lane Hotel Valet Shop, 2842 N. Sheridan Rd., BI 8-1020. Leo Rubin is your friendly neighborhood tailor whose alterations on men's and women's clothes are the equal of Sam Kail's. Big difference in prices, however—Leo's are reasonable. He also presses on the premises, sends out clothes for dry cleaning.

Harry The Shirt Maker, 6142 N. Damen, 338-0656. Mr. Hirschel also turns collars or puts new ones on old shirts, shortens sleeves, etc. Saks Fifth Avenue Men's Shop is one of his customers.

DRESSMAKERS & SEAMSTRESSES

Josi's, 161 E. Grand, MI 2-4514. Josi is one of the most accommodating dress-makers imaginable. Her services include hems and other alterations, reweaving, tailoring, restyling, and she can ably handle leathers and suedes.

Iren, 17 N. State, AN 3-6295. A fantastic old-couturier type whose well-dressed customers swear by her.

Lulu Moore, 7341 S. University, 955-8089. Mrs. Moore is a jewel who comes to your home to do mending; if you have a sewing machine, she'll also sew.

Monogram Embroidery Co., 63 E. Adams, WE 9-3647. Mrs. Adolph Callner and her ladies can monogram anything.

SHOE & HANDBAG REPAIR

Alex, 154 E. Erie, MI 2-3569. Alex Grygowski specializes in custom work—dyeing, respraying leather shoes and handbags, rebuilding, remodeling, orthopedic adjustments. He also covers shoes in your own fabrics and makes shoes to order. His workmanship is elegant; he's so well known you can't expect anything in a hurry.

Zoes, 17 N. State, AN 3-8173. All standard shoe repairs plus restyling and dyeing. Also handbag repair.

Brooks, 111 N. Wabash, FR 2-2504. Major repairs, remodeling; even lowers vamps and converts street shoes to golf shoes. Tints and dyes leathers and fabrics. Also custom-made and orthopedic corrections. Pickup, delivery, and mail order.

Capitol Handbag Co., 55 E. Washington, AN 3-6430. Bring expensive handbags in need of repair here.

Schultz & Mark, 25 E. Washington, CE 6-1156. Makes, repairs, and duplicates fine handbags, including petit point and needlepoint.

REWEAVING, REPAIRS OF FINE CLOTHES & MATERIALS

Josephine Wilkins, 1139 Lunt, RO 4-3601. Miss Wilkins' repair work on wools, linens, laces, and tapestries is extraordinary. She also has little old ladies all over the country with skills nobody else has today. She works out of her home, so phone ahead.

Lillian Boling, 6226 S. Eberhart, 667-4651. Miss Boling is Miss Wilkins' assistant, but she also does reweaving and darning on her own. She meets you at an appointed spot downtown to pick up work.

Marshall Field & Co., 111 N. State, ST 1-1000. If the experts in the dry cleaning department (p. 96) decide they can reweave something, the work will be perfect.

FINE JEWELRY & WATCH REPAIR

Spaulding & Co., 959 N. Michigan, DE 7-4800. The city's outstanding jewelers do beautiful repair work—fairly costly—on fine jewelry, watches, desk and traveling clocks. They also clean and polish gold and platinum jewelry and precious stones, restore damaged sterling, electroplate and refinish silver plate.

C.D. Peacock, State & Monroe, CE 6-0065. As reliable as Spaulding's. Excellent watch and jewelry repair.

Marshall Field & Co., Main Floor Repair Desk, 111 N. State, ST 1-1000. Watches, fine jewelry, good costume jewelry, handbags, and odd things like the tortoiseshell in your great-grandmother's lace fan.

Julian's Antique Jewelry, 25 E. Washington, RA 6-9184. Repairs and remodels all kinds of good jewelry and does custom work. Prices are so reasonable you can't believe them. The amiable owner also buys old gold and jewelry.

Costume Jewelry House, 17 N. State, ST 2-7810. Repairs damaged costume jewelry, repolishes scratched stones, replaces missing stones, changes earring backs, replaces compact mirrors, etc. The owner can be maddening, but he apparently has a corner on this service, so there you are.

CLOCK REPAIR

Smith's Clock Shop, 6241 N. Broadway, AM 2-6151. Painstaking work at reasonable prices.

Chicago Clock, 22 W. Madison, CE 6-5100. Another good place to know about.

Standard Clock Service, 2281 Westview Dr., Des Plaines, VA 4-7063. Conrad Utecht, Jr., repairs grandfather clocks, mantle chimes, Telechron motor clocks and provides Herschede and Revere service.

OPTICAL REPAIR

The top firms for eyeglass and contact lens repair are:

Almer Coe Optical Co., 10 N. and 666 N. Michigan

House of Vision, 135 N. Wabash, 30 N. and 700 N. Michigan

Uhlemann Custom Opticians, 65 E. Washington and Prudential Plaza

The above have additional locations (see "Opticians" in *Yellow Pages B*).

Chevalier, 8 S. Wabash, AN 3-1222. A patient, gentle, knowledgeable guy does optical work "the way I'd want someone to do it for me."

ELECTRONIC, CAMERA, & TYPEWRITER REPAIR

For honest, reliable repair of stereo hi-fi's, phonographs, amplifiers, tape recorders and decks, TVs, aerials, antennas, radios, fans, lamps:

Cherf's TV Sales & Service, 3149 N. Broadway, DI 8-5533. You can ask owner Frank Cherf: "Should I junk this?" and trust his answer. House calls on short appointment.

American Audio Service, 1132 S. Wabash, 427-8330. Repairs tape recorders, phonographs, amplifiers, sound projectors, movie cameras, radios.

Martroy Electronics, 3105 W. 63rd, 778-2898. Repairs radios, TVs, tape recorders, turntables.

Standard Photo Supply Co., 43 E. Chicago, SU 7-3124. Repairs expensive cameras and professional equipment.

Charles W. Mayher & Son, 5 S. Wabash, DE 2-7957. Bring defective binoculars, antique mercury barometers, telescopes with refracting lenses here.

Ritt's Typewriter & Adding Machine Service, 1451 W. Belmont, BU 1-2187. The owner would far rather repair an old metal World War II model than let you trade in for a newer one made mainly of plastics.

HOUSE & HOUSEHOLD SERVICES

Ask for the possibilities, not merely the cheapest way of making repairs. Also realize that service people have to estimate high to protect themselves.

Boilers. People's Gas cleans boilers and room heaters, does general inspection. Adjusts gas appliances and pilot lights for minimum fee of $9. Other services are much more costly. For service offices, look in *Chicago A*.

Bricklayer. Richard M. Schmidt, 3358 N. Southport, BU 1-6067. Fine old German workmanship in tuck-pointing and laying stone, common brick, face brick, firebrick, glass brick.

Contractor. Dominic Venturi Builders, 1529 Sunset Dr., Highland Park, 432-1771. Mr. Venturi not only is willing to build anything from a house to all kinds of small things but has wide resources for odd one-of-a-kind jobs, like building a metal tray to hold plants.

Contract Decorators. Joseph Nimrod Decorating Co., 7055 N. Clark, BR 4-2025. Interior and exterior painting, wall washing, papering, wallpaper removal, cork wall installation, etc. Crews are fast, neat, good at mixing uncommon colors, pleasant—they'll even watch the baby if you have to run to school to retrieve a sick youngster. **Theo Ebert & Co.,** 830 W. Diversey, 281-4770. Interior and exterior work. Fine reputation.

Electric. Liberty Electric, 151 W. Chicago, DE 7-5727, nights 766-0875. Contractors specializing in wiring, repairs, alterations, exterior and interior installations (including chandeliers). Will even create outlets. Figure $18 per hour 8 AM-4:30 PM; time and a half after 4:30 (24-hour service). **Otto Pomper,** 134 S. Dearborn, FR 2-0881. Repairs toasters, irons, coffee makers, shavers, other small appliances. Also sharpens knives and scissors on wheel, all water-ground. **Art's Repair,** 243 W. North, 337-1600. Arthur Guth fixes hand vacuums and other appliances, does wiring, fixes TVs. He knows what he's doing.

Exterminator. Aerosol Exterminators, 4674 N. Elston, PE 6-8118. Guarantees year-round protection on service-contract basis against household pests, including ticks and fleas brought in by dog (take dog to veterinarian). Service to city and suburbs. Mosquito spraying with safe chemicals.

Furniture Rental. Swingles, 320 W. Ohio, 944-6350. Instant furnishings—even lamps—until your own stuff arrives. Probably the best solution in Chicago for newly separated men but be prepared to fight for exactly what you want.

Knife Sharpening. Corrado Cutlery, 26 N. Clark, 368-8450, and 33 E. Adams, 332-2965. **Moon's Grinding & Sharpening Service,** 1012 W. Diversey, 549-7924. Extremely reasonable—30-50¢ depending on size.

Light Bulb Service. Get up to 10 light bulbs in standard sizes free from Commonwealth Edison, 72 W. Adams, 294-8179, by showing your current paid light bill. For other exchange centers, see "Electric Companies" in *Yellow Pages B.*

Locksmiths. A-Act Locksmiths, 3401 N. Clark, GR 2-6079, if no answer 929-3844. A quality outfit, bonded and insured, with 24-hour service. Door locks, padlocks, safes opened and repaired. Also changes combinations and makes keys. Service charge $20 after midnight, $25 on Sunday. **Roy W. Miller,** 9756 S. Mead, Oak Lawn, 424-6953. Does all of above. Also makes keys for cars and antique locks, fits antique keys, and installs door checks. He's busy —you have to keep after him.

Moving Company. Ploegman & Sons, 5115 Cermak, Cicero, OL 2-2400. Takes personal interest in moving you from one part of Chicago to another. In an overpriced field, its charges are fairly reasonable.

Plumbers. T.F. Brown, 114 N. Halsted, FR 2-2996. Faithful, reliable, and with a personal interest in your plumbing. Even tries to explain it to you. **Linstedt,** 3606 N. Southport, LA 5-0637. Plumbing and heating. Also remodels kitchens, bathrooms.

Window Washer. Ruben Arcia, 3559 W. McLean, 276-1730. Washes windows inside and out, takes down screens and washes them, etc. Mainly Near North Side and North Shore.

HONEST CAR REPAIR

Bailey Collision Shop, 601 N. Waller (5700 west), CO 1-0506. A family operation dating from 1903 when wagon repair was as important as car repair. Bodywork is beautiful—cars returned to classic condition. Ask for Charlie or Bruce.

Casten Auto Body Shop, 1130 W. Diversey, 281-5230. Efficient bodywork. Charges always seem appropriate to work done.

K-C Auto Construction, 3276 N. Milwaukee, 283-6433. Fine body shop and motor tune-up. Very reasonable.

Kadlac's Auto Service, 7346 S. Exchange, RE 1-4333. Motor tune-up, brakes, clutches, carburetors. No bodywork.

Standard Service Center, 1600 W. Van Buren, 733-9840. Fine motor tune-up at a Standard Oil station and just about anything else you need. Ask for Frank or Bill.

Erie-LaSalle Body Shop, 148 W. Erie, DE 7-3903. Excellent body shop and fender work, painting.

ARCO Station, 665 N. Dearborn, SU 7-8164. Complete repair shop open weekdays, weekends, nights. Ask for Vince.

Lake Forest Shell Service, 281 E. Illinois, Lake Forest, 234-0202. Good North Shore spot for minor repairs.

Totoh Co., 2911 N. Halsted, 525-4177. Specializes in foreign and sports car work, including domestic sports cars. Most of the dedicated owner-drivers of Rolls, Ferraris, Jaguars bring their jewels here, insist that no one can do more for an engine in a tune-up job.

Jacobs Auto Upholstery, 2959 W. Lawrence, IR 8-4433. If shop doesn't have what you need, it goes out of its way to repair what you've got.

Duxler Firestone Tires, 1225 W. Morse, 761-8550. Open evenings. Reasonable prices and nice people—they'll even put on the spare you didn't buy from them.

24-HOUR GAS STATIONS

Central. Standard stations at 1004 S. Desplaines; Congress & Dearborn; LaSalle & Ontario; North & LaSalle. Shell stations at Ohio & LaSalle; Ontario & Dearborn. ARCO station at 665 N. Dearborn.

North & Northwest. Shell stations at 1160 W. Diversey; 1525 W. North; 1400 W. Division. Standard stations at Fullerton & Seminary; Diversey & California (off Kennedy Expy); Ashland & Lawrence; Touhy & Western; Sheridan & Devon. Mobil station at Pulaski & Irving Park.

West. Standard station at 2955 W. Harrison.

South & Southwest. B & F Service at 52nd & Lake Park. Shell stations at 24 E. 18th; 3501 S. State; 5450 S. Wells; 368 E. Garfield; 8259 S. State. Standard stations at 1600 S. Michigan; 6301 S. Cicero; 7448 S. Stony Island. Patterson Bros. Service Center at 122 E. 103rd.

Suburbs. Shell station at 6400 N. Lincoln (Lincolnwood). Standard stations on Rte. 14 (Northwest Hwy) & Chicago Av. (Palatine); Willow & Shermer (Northbrook); Busse Hwy & Greenwood (Elk Grove Village); Rte. 83 & St. Charles Rd. (Elmhurst); Rte. 83 & 75th St. (Clarendon Hills); Chicago Heights Car Repair Clinic, Rte. 30 & Hilltop (Chicago Heights); S & H Service Station, Sibley (Rte. 83) at Calumet Expy (Dolton).

INSURANCE

Automobile. Rates here are the third highest in the country. Getting auto insurance is rough; it's based on a driver's age, prior driving experience, number of moving violations, whether the car is used for business or pleasure, and where it's garaged. Garaging hasn't to do with carport vs. enclosed space but with location. The Insurance Rating Board divides this city into four areas according to theft ratios, collision, and liability. All three conditions peak in the area bounded by Chicago Av., 47th St., the lake, and Central Av.

Normally, you may carry out-of-state insurance to your policy expiration date—if the company doesn't know about it. If you want to reinsure through your back-home broker, he's obligated to inform the insuring company of change of address, and he then must reinsure at the Chicago rate.

Homeowner's or Tenant's Policies. Type of construction, location, and fire department classification of your building determine rates. Some examples:

1. The building is more than 50 years old, a gracious old brownstone, say, that's been converted from a single family home into apartments. If it has old wiring and old plumbing and both are overworked, expect trouble getting adequate insurance. Shop around to find a broker who can get an insurance company to write coverage.

2. The building is a new high rise located in the area of Chicago's choicest real estate—near or on North Michigan Av. or Lake Shore Dr., north to Belmont Av. It's filled with the people who have the most money, do the most traveling, and who have a constant stream of visitors, domestics, workmen, in and out. Regardless of how different your life-style may be from theirs, you're trapped by their life-style and may have to accept $1,000 deductible on any loss of jewelry or furs. Or you may have to install a safe in your apartment and agree to a clause that no jewelry is covered unless stolen from that safe.* Ah, chic.

---

* Sears puts out acceptable safes. One is labeled "Sears' Underwriters' Lab. Class C Floor Safe." It's roughly $23 \times 18 \times 24$ in., weighs 190 lbs. empty, costs $140. It won't stop a determined professional but will stop an inexperienced filcher or somebody who has access to your apartment because neither can easily cart it off—if at all. Many old apartments have wall safes, but insurance companies don't like them because a pro can open one in 15 minutes flat.

3. You're young, single, and you share an apartment in a highly transient area like the Rush St. area, Old Town, New Town, or Rogers Park near Pratt & Sheridan Rd. Or you're married, you both work, you live in one of the above areas or even a suburban development of singles and young working couples. Housebreaking and burglary are to be expected in neighborhoods that empty daily. Try to get a tenant's policy. Nobody will give you burglary insurance, and fire insurance alone is scarcely adequate.

Jewelry, Furs. If you need large amounts of insurance on these, the policy will have to be divided among several local firms on a pro rata basis, say 25% to each firm, or failing that, submitted to Lloyd's of London. Any single piece of jewelry in excess of $7,000 or several pieces in excess of $25,000 fit the above description.

Note: Condominium ownership creates special insurance problems. Discuss with your broker.

Insurance Agents & Brokers. Homeowner and tenant policies vary from state to state. Your old agent probably can't arrange out-of-state insurance because he's not licensed to write it in Illinois. Ask him for a list of brokers* in Chicago who handle insurance for the company that's been insuring you. Or, if your insuring firm has an office here, call and ask for names of two or three local brokers.

Marsh & McLennan, Inc., 222 S. Riverside Plaza, 648-6000, is one of the few large firms of insuring brokers that will take personal accounts.

Noonan Insurance Service, Inc., 175 W. Jackson, 822-7918, is a small firm noted for the amount of personal attention it gives every client.

If you're black and would prefer to buy insurance from a black company, try **Robbin Insurance Agency,** 8224 S. King Dr., 783-6060.

You can buy insurance direct from Allstate or State Farm and save a little money, but their employees change so often you end up being just one more insured person, and you aren't likely to get much individual attention when you most want it.

---

*You want a broker because a broker not only acts as your representative and determines your needs but is free to go to any company for the best insurance policy he can get for you. An agent represents one or more companies by contract and will sell their insurance only.

CHAPTER VII

PARENTS' GUIDE TO SCHOOLS

You can look at the Chicago public school system in one of two ways:
  A. As a disaster to be fled
  B. As an inadequate ox of a school system* with a few good schools plus a few more capable of reform
The difference in viewpoints is this:

Viewpoint A means you put your children in private schools—or you move to the suburbs.

Viewpoint B means you're willing to make a singular effort to get your children into one of the city's few good public schools. You look for housing near one of these, or you try to enroll your child in one of the city's rare experimental public schools like Disney Magnet or Metropolitan High School which do not limit enrollment to narrow geographical school district boundaries. For uncommon, experimental, and above-average schools, see p. 109.

ADVISORY COUNCILS

No matter where you enroll your child, your interest in his education cannot stop at enrollment. You make a continuing effort to further improve his education by working actively as a member of his school's Parent Advisory Council.

The Parent Advisory Council may be named something else: Community Advisory Council, Advisory Council, Education Council, or the like. Whatever, it is not to be confused with the PTA. Parent advisory council members are drawn from the community—local merchants and businessmen, clergymen of different denominations, parents, teachers, usually the school principal.

A typical advisory council has 12-18 members; at least 60% must be parents of children in the school. Though it can't fire a principal, an advisory council can exert great pressure on the Board of Education and the superintendent of schools and force the transfer of an unsatisfactory principal. It can also pressure the Board of Education to provide funds for a jeopardized special-reading program. It can refuse a program offered by the Board of Education, or if the Board makes choices available, nominate its choice—for instance, the 12-months-of-school plan with one of its four options.

Theoretically, an advisory council cannot force the Board of Education to install language classes for Spanish-speaking children—but in at least one

---

*Among its problems: yearly money crises; gross segregation; strike-prone Chicago Teachers Union; citizen apathy; on-again-off-again press, and above all, a conservative and ineffective school board (members appointed by the mayor—Mayor Daley has a *McGuffey's Reader* attitude about education).

instance, an advisory council did just that and got the TESL program (Teaching English as a Second Language) for its school.

An advisory council can raise funds for needed school equipment and be innovative in seeking funds for special programs. It can run circles around a PTA in many instances because of its inherent power. Though a great many parent advisory councils won't use the power because of the time and work involved, one person's willingness to assume almost heroic leadership can effect change.

A Chicago public school *can* provide effective education when it has a courageous, innovative principal backed by a like-minded school district superintendent and a like-minded parent advisory council that will also pitch in.

Backing means willingness to let a principal and his teachers experiment with curriculum and teaching methods. Pitching in means willingness to tackle the Board of Education and keep after it until it provides what's needed.

Not easy, but it can be done. You have to give endless hours of time and energy to a school and its problems, to other parents and their problems, and to the question of what contemporary education must be if it's going to educate your child and his classmates.

All this presupposes a fairly stable, mainly middle-class neighborhood. In neighborhoods undergoing vast change, the quality of schools can change drastically in a matter of a year or two. In a fringe neighborhood where young professional families are moving in, their influence, coupled with tremendous effort and a super principal, just might upgrade a school. Some very hip young parents join a parent advisory council before their first child is ready to be enrolled in a school—that's another way to be in a position of some power at the time one's child starts his formal education.

What it all adds up to is a potential for a kind of consumer education movement that's barely been tapped. Parent advisory councils in Chicago are new—Supt. of Schools James F. Redmond created them only in 1970. Too few parents have grasped their significance. Too few councils are anywhere near as functional as they could be. Obviously they cannot offset fundamental problems such as too-large schools or the need for decentralization. But since they're one rare hope in an otherwise almost hopeless situation, they ought to be worked for all they're worth.

GUIDELINES FOR TRANSFEREES

If you're being transferred to Chicago and must make a fast housing decision based on public schools, opt for the suburbs. Obviously, some suburban public schools are better than others, but all attract young teachers, invest heavily in teaching aids, and strain for curriculum development.

If the advantages of city living are what you want, use the guidelines for evaluating public schools below. Also see "Chicago's Uncommon, Experimental, & Above-Average Public Schools," p. 109-111.

Can you judge schools on the basis of National Merit Scholarships? Not really. National Merit tests measure individual achievement, not schools. Furthermore, 15,000 high school students on a nationwide basis qualify annually as Semifinalists—yet National Merit has only 3,400 scholarships to award. Thus, the only useful figures—and only semiuseful at that—are Semifinalist lists of schools that somewhat consistently turn out students with some measurable basis of achievement. Education Dept., Chicago Public Library, Randolph & Michigan, maintains yearly lists of Chicago and suburban schools graduating Merit Scholarship Semifinalists.

EVALUATING A CHICAGO PUBLIC SCHOOL

If you want to live in Chicago, want to send your child to a public school, and want to find the "best" school, here's what you do:

Call the Board of Education, 641-4141. Ask for the head of the Dept. of Operations Analysis. Say that you have a child entering public school and would like to know something about the schools in your area. Ask if the current edition of *Selected School Characteristics* can be mailed to you. It's bulky and hard to handle, but it gives statistical information on the quality of individual schools. Schools are grouped by district, and better schools will be grouped together. "Better" refers to the four criteria below. These will help you decide if you ought to make the effort to get your child into a private or parochial school. If *Selected School Characteristics* isn't available, find at Board of Education Library, 228 N. LaSalle, or Chicago Public Library.

The Chicago public school system classifies schools as follows: child-parent centers (for certain poverty areas), elementary schools, upper-grade centers (grades 7-8), general high schools, technical high schools, vocational high schools, and special schools for physically handicapped children. For information on any of these categories, call Board of Education.

Check the following. Does a school you're interested in have:
1. Low student-teacher ratio (essential in elementary school)
2. High percentage of teachers with 6-15 years experience and high percentage with master's degrees plus 30 graduate hours beyond master's degree
3. Special programs such as *special reading classes*, TESL (Teaching English as a Second Language), classes for handicapped, etc.
4. High per-pupil staffing cost. The higher the cost per pupil, the more and better experienced the teachers

Board of Education also publishes a 600-page book, *Report of the City-Wide Testing Program*, that contains group achievement test data. Tests are national; reading scores reflect the median percentile rank based on national standardization samples. Available at Board of Education Library, Chicago Public Library, or any school principal's office.

After narrowing school possibilities, start talking to people who live in the school district, to parents who have children in the school, to a shopkeeper, to the cop on the corner, to anyone. Then drop in on the school—during the lunch hour. That's when the discipline and educational process at any school begin to break down and you can see what's really happening at gut level.

Getting into a Chicago public school isn't easy. Politely insist that as a taxpayer you have a right to enter, that as a parent you have the same right. You may need a special pass, but it can usually be obtained in the main office. If you continue to meet resistance, go to someone on the parent advisory council.

As you walk through halls toward the lunchroom, watch the students. Are they going somewhere, or are they just hanging around? Look at walls. What do the graffiti tell you? Are they rough or are they innocuous like "Lucy + George"?

If you're not easily intimidated, go into a washroom. Is it filled with large groups of kids who seem to have been hanging around for hours? Has it enough towels, toilet paper, supplies? Excuse a reasonable amount of mess, and try to figure out when the room was last cleaned.

Is the lunchroom fairly orderly? (Ignore noise level—it's bound to be high.) Does the food seem edible? Are smaller children supervised? Are the tables fairly clear or clean? (Later, check to see if the school has an adequate lunch program.)

Talk to a few students. What do they think of the school? What's good about it, what's not? Do any of their friends go to another school that's better? Why is the other school better? Don't worry about having to discount youthful prejudices. Youngsters are often fairly conservative when you ask such general questions—unless someone has just browbeaten them. Certainly they have a bias, but it's usually no greater than that of the faculty or the principal or the policeman in the lunchroom.

If you happen upon a friendly teacher, ask if you may see what the class is doing. Try to sit in on a few classes. If this takes the cooperation of the principal, ask him for permission. Realize he'll probably send you to one of his better teachers. Your child might have one of the worst, so once he's enrolled, check with his teacher.

Visit the playground at recess—it's full of revelations. It shows you the entire school population, allows you to estimate the racial and ethnic population of the school. You can see the way the children interact—whether they're running wild (a potential for violence) or playing together. You can learn about staff supervision here, and at dismissal, you can learn something about the parents who come to pick up their children.

Stay in touch with what your child thinks of his teacher and what the teacher thinks of your child. This takes much reading between the lines but is worth an active effort. A teacher pays more attention to a child whose parents bother to come to school to talk about him.

Remember, the key to a good school is the principal—one who is realistic about the kinds of youngsters he's dealing with, knows what they need to complement the informal education they receive in the community. Ask what he thinks are his school's greatest problems. Does he have advanced placement classes and classes for handicapped children and slow learners? What kinds of programs does the school sponsor that give students an awareness of their community?

Is the principal aware of the way(s) courses in his school are taught? Does he know the conservative and liberal factions of his staff? Does he seem to develop new ideas brought to him by his staff? Is he giving you a snow job?

A really good principal is willing to talk but won't have all day. Try to ask pertinent questions that can't be brushed off with pacifying answers; rely heavily on your gut reaction. To learn if a principal does what he says he does, go to parent advisory council meetings and talk to teachers and parents who seem to be involved. Most are, or they wouldn't be there. Duck the one who has an obvious ax to grind.

Give a public school a plus if it's located near a college or university and has students whose parents are affiliated with the university. The university may have injected the school with some of its viable new ideas on education, thus eliminating the usual 20-year lag.*

CHICAGO'S UNCOMMON, EXPERIMENTAL, & ABOVE-AVERAGE PUBLIC SCHOOLS

William B. Ogden Elementary School, 24 W. Walton, 787-6102. Innovative, interracial, small enrollment (500), wonderfully diverse student mix. Near North Side location brings in children of Chicago's consular corps, children from upper-middle-income families, children from ADC families (40% of school population is below poverty level). Ogden has two special-education programs and that rarity—a school band. A dedicated principal, good age-mix staff, and intense parent involvement (Parent Advisory Council and active PTA) create driving forces for the school. Staff and parents unusually aggressive in seeking new funding sources to provide special programs.

Walt Disney Magnet School, 4140 N. Marine Dr., 525-3731. An experimental school affiliated with Northwestern University though not near it. As a magnet school, Disney accepts pupils from entire north section of the city from an irregular south boundary that wiggles between Madison and 12th Sts. north to the city limits. Students are computer-selected so that the school achieves a racial, ethnic, and sex mix (50% boys, 50% girls). Ages 3-13 accepted. Open classrooms, ungraded programs, a total laboratory school environment. Disney goals for students are like those of the best private schools; faculty encourages original thinking and independence. Separate Communication Arts Center, with own staff, used by non-Disney children† throughout city after school hours and by young adults and adults at night.

Lewis Wirth Experimental Branch of Kenwood High School, 4959 S. Blackstone, KE 6-3100. For grades 6-7-8. The only public school literally created by parents—that is, dissatisfied parents gave the Board of Education a report stating what kind of school they wanted, and the school was created in 1969. Individualized programs include accelerated classes and electives for all students, learning labs, language choice—French, Spanish, or German. Wirth students with low success in academic subjects allowed to take classes in which they can excel (shop, say, or band) simultaneously at Kenwood High School next door—success in the latter stimulates achievement in the former. Student population: 400, 87% black.

---

* A lag exists between the time an effective educational innovation is proved in independent schools and knowledge of it or its use filters down to the average public school teacher.

† If you're a working mother, investigate as an after-school possibility for your children.

Kenwood High School, 5015 S. Blackstone, 538-3538. Is an advanced learning center, has a superior curriculum, is big on field trips, and is located in Hyde Park-Kenwood, where proximity to the University of Chicago makes a difference. Its student body is integrated (67% black) and can be rough to the degree that you'll have to teach a freshman son or daughter how to handle casual invitations to couple. Innovative electives for seniors include choice of four mini-courses such as Alienation of the Adolescent in Fiction, Theatre of the Absurd, Old Testament Literature, Movie Appreciation, African Literature. Also college-level courses including calculus and computer sciences.

Albert G. Lane Technical High School, 2501 W. Addison, 935-7208. Originally a technical high school, Lane has broadened its base to become a college-preparatory school. It offers courses uncommon in Chicago public high schools—Russian, pre-engineering, pre-architecture, college prep for majors in music, math, science, etc. Some 85% of Lane's graduates go to college. Admission by formal application (make while in elementary school). Students must have an IQ of 100 or higher, must bring a report card showing competence, must have a good attendance record and a recommendation from their principal. Children of newcomers to Chicago can make late applications. Student population: 4,800 boys, 600 girls, 91% white. Lane accepts students from 12th St. north to city limits.

Robert Lindblom High School, 6130 S. Wolcott, 436-2501. Not quite the same caliber as Lane but works toward being the South Side equivalent. Student body is 94% black.

Metropolitan High School, 537 S. Dearborn, 939-3141. Probably the most experimental public school in the city. Basically college preparatory (no trade or vocational training offered). Students have definite voice in curriculum, teacher selection, courses they want to take. Majority of classes take place outside the school, hence nickname "school-without-walls." School works best for independent, fairly mature students. Admission by lottery drawing.

Also worth investigating

In the Lincoln Park area, **Lincoln Elementary School,** 615 W. Kemper Pl., has opened itself to the community, encourages parental help with school projects and workshops that enrich the basic education program. **Oscar Mayer Elementary School,** 2250 N. Clifton, is trying to use the community, and the community insists on input.

When you find a school that discourages community involvement, as some do, figure it's too rigid for your child's education and look elsewhere.

Look into **Mather High School** feeder schools in West Ridge and west section of Rogers Park. Students at Mather, 5835 N. Lincoln, come mainly from highly motivated Jewish families, and the motivation is evident in school performance. Board of Education will supply names and addresses of the feeder schools.

Investigate feeder schools for **Sullivan High School,** 6631 N. Bosworth. Sullivan's location in east Rogers Park is in a multiracial, multi-socioeconomic community.

Look into feeder schools for **Von Steuben High School,** 5039 N. Kimball.

On the Near South Side, investigate the integrated, well-regarded South Commons Branch of **Drake Elementary School,** 2722 S. King Dr.

In Hyde Park-Kenwood, investigate **Bret Harte,** 1556 E. 56th, and **Ray,** 5631 S. Kimbark. Both are elementary schools feeding into **Kenwood High School.**

In Beverly Hills-Morgan Park, **Kellogg Elementary,** 9241 S. Leavitt, annually ranks first in city test scores. **Sutherland Elementary,** 10015 S. Leavitt, is similar. Both feed into **Morgan Park High School,** 1744 W. Pryor. Morgan Park has problems, but it also has a dynamic principal and a staff challenged by problems. Programs are exciting, staff reaches for excellence at all levels.

INDEPENDENT (PRIVATE) & PAROCHIAL SCHOOLS

For the most part, Chicago's private schools rank with the best in the country. At least four—Francis W. Parker, The Harris School, The Latin School, and The University of Chicago Laboratory Schools—are prestigious. All private schools here emphasize individualized instruction, allow each student as much time and practice as necessary to master specific goals.

Until recently, Chicago's largely Roman Catholic parochial schools were traditionally authoritarian and heavily church-oriented. Change came because they've had to fight for their lives, hence unusual programming and innovative curriculum. A few of the most innovative are included here. To learn about others, contact **Catholic School Board,** 527-3200. Ask for *Catholic School Directory* and *The Grand Design.*

For parochial schools affiliated with other religious denominations, check your pastor or phone **Church Federation of Greater Chicago,** 372-2427. The Federation can supply denominational office phone numbers. If you want a college-preparatory school, ask the parochial school office what percentage of graduates go to college, how many win scholarships, how many drop out.

Figure tuition at private or parochial schools as $300 to more than $2,000 annually.* Most schools are near the higher figure because that's what it costs to educate a child for one year. None of the schools are making a profit.

Enrollment varies from less than 200 to nearly 3,000. Average enrollment is about 500 students. For comparison, public high school enrollment averages 2,000 students per school. Teacher-student ratio in independent schools is 1:6 to 1:17. In public schools it can be as high as 1:38.

Most private and parochial schools use entrance tests, give scholarships, are struggling financially despite high tuition rates. Most have teachers who must be dedicated to something since they earn less in independent schools than they could in public schools. At worst, a teacher may be dedicated to elitism or resistance to required education courses for accreditation to public school teaching. Mainly, these teachers are dedicated to trying new ideas, to working in a system responsive to each student's needs.

Private and parochial schools pride themselves on a sense of community. Alumni are welcomed back, parents are invited in. The most disparaging comment that can be made about some of these schools is that they're cliqu-

---

* Plus fees for books, lunches, uniforms if required, etc. At a school like Latin, extras can easily run $250 yearly. At some private schools, parents are also pressured into almost mandatory tax-deductible contributions, say $200 annually.

ish. Generally, though, you and your child feel at home in the school.

Accreditation: usually by North Central Assn. of Secondary Schools and/or National Assn. of Independent Schools. However, The Latin School has resisted accrediting for years on the grounds that certain requirements governing course selection and faculty hiring are too restrictive.

Academy of the Sacred Heart for Girls, 6250 N. Sheridan Rd., AM 2-4446. Grades 1-8 and 9-12. Run by the Religious of the Sacred Heart, but 84% of faculty are lay teachers, and 20-25% of students are not Catholic. Girls come from all over city but mainly North Side. French begins in first grade. First four grades use British primary system of integrated day, with classrooms divided into specially equipped areas for science, math, language arts, visual arts. High school offers alternative to traditional A-B-C-D-F grading whereby progress is evaluated by student and teacher. Extensive use of city resources. Qualified students take college courses at nearby Mundelein College, receive credits at both levels. Tuition $800-1,000.

Ancona School, 4770 S. Dorchester, 924-2356. Elementary, coed Montessori school for ages 6-11. All races, religions, ethnic groups from entire South Side. Program is nongraded, open classrooms, innovative. Contrary to some popular belief, there is no religious education except information-only kind. Children with prior Montessori experience given preferential but not exclusive consideration for admission. Tuition $1,150 plus a one-time $200 loan to the school for duration of a child's enrollment. Ancona is a not-for-profit corporation owned cooperatively by parents. For nursery school, see p. 116.

Note: Illinois Montessori Society, P.O. Box 735, Oak Park, Ill. 60303, 582-8890, will mail a list of Illinois Montessori schools but will not make recommendations.

Anshe Emet Day School, 3760 N. Pine Grove, BU 1-1423. Nursery (age 3) through grade 8, coed. Traditional American private school education with 20% of day given to Hebrew and Bible studies (started in kindergarten with puppets). Non-Jewish and black pupils welcome but must take religious curriculum. Tuition $725-1,200.

Faulkner School, 7110 S. Coles, BA 1-3578. Coed, kindergarten through grade 12. All races, religions, ethnic groups. Program basically traditional college preparatory. French begins in first grade. Tuition $750-1,725.

Gordon Technical High School, 3633 N. California, KE 9-3600. For boys, grades 9-12. Run by the Resurrectionist Fathers, but 75% of faculty are lay teachers. Admission preference given Catholics (all but 2% of students are). Despite name, Gordon is now a comprehensive school offering academic as well as technical and vocational subjects. In 1971, 68% of graduating class went to college, 15% to trade or technical schools, 7% to full-time employment, 5% to apprenticeship programs, 5% to armed forces. Tuition $500.

Hardy Preparatory School for Boys, 6250 N. Sheridan Rd., AM 2-4446. Run by the Religious of the Sacred Heart; the brother elementary school to Academy of the Sacred Heart. Boys come from all over the North Side; 20% are non-Catholic. Headmaster and 50% of the faculty are men; 64% of faculty are lay teachers. Outstanding study-skills program: each student selects an area of interest and follows through with his studies in a tutorial situation. Tuition $800-850.

The Harris School, 541 W. Hawthorne, 348-1530. Kindergarten through high school, nongraded, coed, interracial. Upper School is traditional college preparatory. Conversational French starts in kindergarten. Tuition $950-2,016.

Harvard-St. George School, 4731 S. Ellis, OA 4-0394. Kindergarten through grade 12, coed, interracial. Students mainly from Hyde Park-Kenwood and South Shore, a few from Near North Side. School is humanities-oriented, still offers Latin. High school is college preparatory. Programs include outdoor education week at winter camp, community involvement course, spring camp. Special program for perceptually handicapped children. Tuition $980-1,500.

The Latin School of Chicago, Lower School, 1531 N. Dearborn; Upper School and Office, 59 W. North, 787-0820. Coed from junior kindergarten through grade 12. All races, religions, ethnic groups. Students mostly from North Side. Traditional college preparatory. Among high school electives: calculus, studio art, psychology, film, urban history, civil liberties and the Constitution. Tuition $950-1,880. Special summer program includes both academic and non-academic courses for students who want subjects not offered in winter school: Greek, Latin, cultural anthropology, Russian history, etc.

Near North Montessori School, 1010 W. Chicago, 226-1010. Coed, ages 6-13 in nongraded, innovative, open classrooms. All races, religions, ethnic groups. Students come from North, Near West, and Near South Sides. As at Ancona, no religious instruction; preference for admission given to children with prior Montessori experience. All parents are members of the not-for-profit Montessori School Corp. Tuition $1,100.

Francis W. Parker School, 330 W. Webster, LI 9-0172. The school brochure states that "a school's student body should, as far as possible, represent the elements of a democratic society." Parker makes an extra effort to get a wide coed student mix—racially, ethnically, religiously, economically—from junior kindergarten through grade 12. Students come from entire city. Program is progressive college preparatory, with strong emphasis on the arts. Older students assume an increasing share of planning their own work and the government of the school. Tuition $900-1,820.

St. Ignatius College Preparatory, 1076 W. Roosevelt, 421-5900. For boys, grades 9-12. A Jesuit school with preferential consideration for admission given to Catholics—6% of students are not. Traditional college prep, with exceptional math department. Boys come from entire city. Tuition, including lab fees and equipment, $800.

St. Mary Center for Learning, 2044 W. Grenshaw, 666-4169. Coed high school highly experimental in inner-urban education. Sisters of Charity/BVM community of nuns hope to turn over school operation to a corporation of businessmen and women in community-at-large. Innovative program emphasizes decision making by consensus, community spirit, awareness of self, and value of work—some say to detriment of skills, but students love the learning experience. Students are inner-city mix, though now coming from across city and suburbs: 15% Italian, 30% black, 15% Spanish-speaking, 15% Slavic, 25% Irish-Asian-Jewish-other. Tuition $450.

The University of Chicago Laboratory Schools, 1362 E. 59th, 753-2521. Kindergarten through grade 12. For nursery school, see p. 116. Coed; all races, religions, ethnic groups but predominantly upper middle class. Students come from all over South Side but mainly Hyde Park-Kenwood; some 40-50% are children of U. of C. faculty. French or German started at grade-3 level. High school is progressive college preparatory. High school students may take courses in the college. Tuition $1,000-2,000.

The Van Gorder-Walden School, 721 N. LaSalle, 266-1270. Coed for ages 4-18. New school founded 1973 by Dr. Edwin Van Gorder, recent headmaster of The Latin School. Innovative, college preparatory. The youngest students spend class day in open classroom approach to learning; all others spend three hours daily in intensive individualized study of English and math (very broadly defined), then in highly individualized curriculum. School uses Chicago as a vast resource center and a farm in Wisconsin to provide rural boarding-learning experience. Nonprofit, nondenominational. Actively seeks students of all racial and ethnic backgrounds. Tuition $1,000-1,950. Some scholarships available.

Note: Neither Illinois nor Chicago requires that schools be accredited, hence the growing number of "free" or "alternate" schools. These schools have problems, not the least of which is their fluidity. If you're interested in them, you have to develop your own ideas about the kind of education you want your child to have and be able to size up a free school to see if it achieves its goals. Because their life-span averages 18 months, none are listed here. American Friends Service Committee, 407 S. Dearborn, 427-2533, keeps track of them with a newsletter, *New School News.*

HIGHER EDUCATION

The two giants among privately funded universities and colleges in the Chicago area are the University of Chicago and Northwestern University.

Next in prestige: Loyola University, Illinois Institute of Technology, DePaul University, University of Illinois at Chicago Circle,* Roosevelt University, and Lake Forest, Barat, and Mundelein Colleges.

For insights into all these, see "Intellectual Oases" in *Chicago: An Extraordinary Guide* by Jory Graham (Rand McNally). Not included in the first edition:

Columbia College, 540 N. Lake Shore Dr., 467-0300. For students intent on careers in one of the public arts—motion picture, photography, broadcasting, journalism, advertising, art/graphics, music, dance, theatre, etc. Curriculum is offbeat, appeals to talented students who care more about training than degrees. Splendid faculty; its members have immediate professional commitment to subjects they teach.

---

* Other state-run universities in the Chicago area: Northeastern Illinois, Chicago State, and Governors State.

Art Institute of Chicago, Adams & Michigan, CE 6-7080, offers four years of fine arts leading to Bachelor of Fine Arts degree.

Note: At least 20 small, private two- and four-year colleges are scattered throughout the Chicago area. For information on these, use the *College Blue Book* in Education Dept., Chicago Public Library, or a suburban library.

For a complete list of all public and private colleges, junior colleges, universities, theological seminaries, private professional schools, and other private institutions, call **State of Illinois Board of Higher Education,** 793-3243, or write Board at 160 N. LaSalle, Chicago 60601.

Chicago operates eight junior colleges plus a TV college. At least ten suburbs have junior colleges but usually call them community colleges. Use *College Blue Book* for these too.

The Learning Exchange, P.O. Box 920, Evanston 60204, 864-4133. New concept in community education outside of schools based on belief that "most people are willing to share what they know with others and that learning, teaching and sharing similar interests can be enjoyable and rewarding." Matches people of all ages, races, sexes, educational backgrounds in Chicago area as teachers or learners to form discussion groups and classes in 850 areas of interest. More than 4,000 members and keeps growing. Phone manned daily, 10 AM to 10 PM. Free, but hopes for tax-deductible contributions from users.

INDEPENDENT NURSERY SCHOOLS

These vary enormously when it comes to programs. Some believe in little or no structure, some in total structure. Most try for flexibility within a structured program. Few will take a child less than two years nine months old except by special permission. A five-year-old is frequently considered a senior kindergartner and as such fits into an elementary school system.

Many nursery schools ask for mother participation at school one session each week or one day each month. If a school is church-operated, admission preference is usually given to children of church members even though no formal religious instruction is presented to the children.

Though independent nursery schools are licensed by Illinois Dept. of Children & Family Services, licensing merely means a school meets minimum physical standards of space, fire regulations, and the like. Hence, a shocking number of so-called nursery schools make no attempt whatsoever to provide essential learning experiences. A nursery school that merely attempts to amuse children is an awful waste of money and probably not what your child needs. The only way to know if a nursery school meets *your* requirements is to visit it. Nursery schools with high standards of their own will welcome you. Eschew those that don't.

If you're new to the nursery school bit, read Maya Pines' *Revolution in Learning* (Harper & Row). Or write National Assn. for the Education of Young Children, 1834 Connecticut Av. NW, Washington, D.C. 20009, for pamphlet *Some Ways of Distinguishing a Good School or Center for Young Children.*

The nursery schools listed here are generally regarded as having the most thoughtful, innovative programs and the happiest little achievers. Make application in February preceding school year you want your child to attend. These schools are always filled to capacity.

Ancona School, 4770 S. Dorchester, 924-2356. A Montessori school. AM and PM groups, ages 3-6. Integrated, nonsectarian. Tuition $670 plus $200 loan to school for each child during his enrollment. Tuition aid available.

Fourth Church Day School (Fourth Presbyterian Church), 115 E. Delaware Pl., 787-4570. AM program for age 3, PM for age 4. Integrated, interracial; one-third of children have parents attending the church. Tuition $650 for members; nonmembers add a $200 contribution to scholarship fund. Tuition aid available.

Home Club Nursery School, 7601 S. Phillips (South Shore Community Center), RE 1-0444. Ages 3-5. Integrated, nonsectarian. Tuition $75 per month for full day, $45 for half day. Tot lot available for ages 1-2½ and their mothers for first experience in playing with other children.

Lincoln Park Cooperative Nursery School, 2335 N. Orchard, 549-7170. AM and PM groups in one of the best-run, most popular co-op nursery schools in city (always four applications for each opening—children admitted in order of application). Tuition based on parents' judgment of what they can afford: $18-38 monthly one child, $28-50 monthly two children. Tuition aid available.

Near North Montessori School, 1010 W. Chicago, 226-1010. AM and PM groups for ages 3-6. Integrated. Draws from wide area. Tuition $800 half day, $900 extended day. Tuition aid available.

The Unitarian Preschool Center (First Unitarian Church), 5650 S. Woodlawn, FA 4-4100. AM and PM groups, mainly ages 3-4 in AM and ages 4-5 in PM. Multiracial, nonsectarian. Tuition $500. Day care program for ages 3-7 (7:30 AM-5:45 PM), $35 weekly. Tuition aid available.

The University of Chicago Nursery School, 5750 S. Woodlawn, 753-2538. Probably the oldest nursery school in the country and nationally recognized as the finest. AM only for ages 3-4. Interracial, nonsectarian. Exceptional teacher-child ratio of 1:7. Some 80% of youngsters are children of U. of C. faculty and staff. Regular tuition $1,000.

Also worth investigating: Lakeview Nursery School at Jane Addams Center, 3212 N. Broadway; Lakeview Tot Lot at same address; Anshe Emet NS (p. 112); Bernard Horwich Jewish Community Center NS, 3003 W. Touhy; Sinai NS, 1720 E. 54th.

Exceptional suburban nursery schools: National College of Education NS, Evanston; Flossmoor Community Church NS; Highland Park Community NS & Day Care Center; Ravinia NS, Highland Park; Winnetka Community NS; Prairie State Child Development Center, Chicago Heights.

DAY CARE CENTERS

Like nursery schools, far too many day care centers give little more than custodial care. Furthermore, there's an appalling dearth of reasonably priced day care centers for middle-class children.

A working mother (or student) who is the sole support of her children may qualify for admission to a federally funded day care center in a poverty neighborhood—assuming availability of federal funds. For instance, Jane Addams Center, 3212 N. Broadway, runs two federally funded centers for children. A few of these youngsters are children of middle-class working mothers; most are children of indigent parents. To learn if you qualify, apply to Chicago Committee on Urban Opportunity, 744-7272, or to Illinois Dept. of Children & Family Services, 341-8494 or 341-8436.

To locate privately owned and operated day care centers in the city or suburbs, contact **Day Care Crisis Council,** 201 N. Wells, 332-1722. It's a citizens watchdog organization that helps groups trying to start day care centers cut through the bureaucratic licensing maze; feeds them technical and financial advice; offers expertise on licensing, staffing, funding, and curriculum development.

But as with nursery schools, licensing means only that a center meets minimum physical requirements. You simply cannot pick a center without visiting it. Look for:

1. Low adult-child ratio—1:5 to 1:7
2. Nice interaction between staff and children—lots of warmth, spontaneity, affection, caring
3. Competent, interested staff—adults more concerned about interacting with children than in talking with visiting adults
4. Encourages parent involvement, welcomes your questions
5. Keeps adequate records of each child's health and progress
6. Uses the services of professional consultants in the field of child development and learning disabilities

Watch the children. Do they seem happy? Are they having fun? Do they have enough room to play? Are they free to ask questions, free to explore? Or are they highly regimented? Is there a hum of activity, or are children sitting passively at little tables?

Two highly qualified, integrated, not-for-profit day care centers are:

Laurance Armour Day School, 630 S. Ashland, 243-6414. Owned by Rush-Presbyterian-St. Luke's Medical Center so admission preference is given to children of medical center staff. Takes children ages 2 through kindergarten, 6:45 AM-5:30 PM. Closed in July. Tuition $125 per month, $70 for half day (includes lunch); also an after-school program for older children, $40 per month. Tuition aid available.

St. Vincent DePaul Center, 2145 N. Halsted, 943-6776. Preschool ages 2-5, school age 6-12. Open 7 AM-6 PM. Professional and volunteer staff. Sliding scale tuition, maximum $50 per week.

Also worth investigating: Hyde Park Neighborhood Club, 5480 S. Kenwood, MI 3-4062; Chatham Preschool, 741 E. 84th, 488-8177 (black); Betty's Nursery & Kindergarten, 1024 E. 83rd, 994-6811 (black); Ezzard Charles School, 6701 S. Emerald, 487-0223 (Montessori, black).

For children with special needs because of learning disabilities, retardation, or emotional disturbances, call **Community Referral Service,** 427-9623. It can help with day care centers, schools, social service agencies—whatever you need.

CHAPTER VIII

MAKING NEW FRIENDS—METHOD A

How do you meet people in a city as vast as Chicago? Here's how: Ask yourself what you enjoy doing that's done in groups. Then find a group or organization with the same interest and join it. That's where people you're likely to enjoy meeting will be. For singles, it's really one of the easiest ways to meet the opposite sex.

Method A for making friends is simply a matter of finding groups that emphasize socializing or creativity. By joining, you not only meet people you can enjoy but enrich your own social or creative potential at the same time.

Method B is for people who want to help improve a little part of society: you join a group that's pushing for your kind of goal. If you're basically shy, a goal-oriented group is exactly the right kind to join because the goal will always be more important than you are.

MORE THAN JUST SOCIAL

Chicago Council on Foreign Relations, 116 S. Michigan, RA 6-3870. Outstanding organization for anyone keenly interested in U.S. foreign policy and world affairs. Weekly programs with speakers of international stature range from lecture-forum series and dinner-seminars in city and suburbs to cocktail parties in attractive places such as the Arts Club. Excellent low-cost travel programs with insider briefings at embassies and consulates.

Council Forum, for ages 20-40, is even more energetic—adventures around the city, holds dinner meetings in ethnic restaurants, Sunday brunch programs, wine tastings, and cocktail parties for pure socializing. This group is one of the best in town if you want to meet eligible attorneys, businessmen and women, teachers, young journalists, and the like.

Membership in Council or Council Forum, $15 single or couple. Try out first by going to a few events, paying nonmember fee.

The Canyon, Inc. Lively luncheon club with speakers on subjects of current interest—political, aesthetic, controversial. Also four or five yearly cocktail parties. Members are mainly single, ages 20-35, in business or professions. Canyon actively seeks new members, but hard-core swingers won't enjoy. Current membership 250. Not yet racially integrated but trying hard to be. Dues $20, include cost of first three luncheons you attend. To see if you'll enjoy, go to a couple of luncheon meetings as a nonmember at $3.50 per. Contact Paul Kimball at his office, FR 2-2900.

AYH, 3712 N. Clark, EA 7-8114. Joining American Youth Hostels is a first-rate way to meet people who thrive on action: backpacking, canoeing, sailing, skiing (downhill and cross-country), folk dancing, cycling (after work, Friday restaurant rides, weekend trips). Instruction offered in all of these. Weekend junkets take you to places you might not easily find on your own. Because activities are substantial, friendships and intimacies can develop without the kind of effort you have to make in singles bars. Trips (very inexpensive) arranged for equal number men and women. Huge membership, mainly in 20s-30s. Interracial—largest number of blacks are in ski club. Dues $11 senior (over 18), $6 junior, $13 family.

The Learning Exchange (p. 115) is a marvelous way to meet people. It can find you a tennis partner, lead you to others who also, say, play the bagpipes, or draw from your own talents and match you to others as a teacher.

Mensa. This one's for people who feel intellectually starved for conversation and ideas. Chicago-area Mensa has 600 members ranging from high IQ dropouts to multiple doctorates. Members are of every conceivable political leaning, every age, every occupation, 60% single. Monthly meeting with speaker at Lake Tower Inn, 600 N. Lake Shore Dr., followed by rap session at member's home. Weekend discussion groups, Loop luncheons, and the like. Would-be members welcome at a couple of meetings before applying for membership (you must be within the top 2% of the population in intelligence and prove it, either by prior record or by taking a standard IQ test, $15). Dues $15, waived if you can't afford to pay. Contact Gene Edlin at his office, 236-3242.

Cercle Universitaire Franco-Américain. One of the happiest interracial, bilingual groups in Chicago for ages 18-35. French is the language spoken, so you find a large number of university students and graduates among the French, American whites and blacks, Haitians, and Arabs in the organization. Lectures, outings, literary discussions, celebration of French holidays, wine tastings. Meets monthly during academic year in various locations including French restaurants. Good place for singles—five marriages in the last couple of years. Membership fee $8 single, $10 couple. Contact French Cultural Service, 664-3525.

Ponte dell'Arte. For people who love Italy and anything Italianate. Season starts in October with events such as parties in art galleries, mini-benefits in a member's home (cash bar, but hostess prepares food, and entertainment follows). Members (about 125) are mix of younger Chicagoans and suburbanites, about as many married as single. Nonmembers welcome at one or two events to test. Dues $10 single, $15 couple. Contact Gabe W. Burton at his home, 307 Wisconsin, WH 3-5548.

Crossroads, 5621 S. Blackstone, MU 4-6060. International, interracial student center open six days weekly to all students, grad researchers, doctors and nurses, wives of students. Regular Friday night panel discussions and Saturday luncheons ($1.25). Also a variety of inexpensive social events and language classes in French, Spanish, German, English. No dues.

Ski Clubs. More than 50 of them in the Chicago area. The way to find one that meets your needs is through the **Chicago Metropolitan Ski Council,** governing body for all ski clubs here. Write P.O. Box 7926, Chicago 60680, or call 544-4627 after 6 PM. Meanwhile, here's an example of one of the most socially active.

Sandburg Ski Club. Huge membership (800) of skiers and nonskiers who show up 200-400 strong for meetings and cash-bar cocktail parties. Equal number men and women, ages mainly 25-35, overwhelmingly single. Meet every other Tuesday at Germania Club, 108 W. Germania. Weekend ski trips in Midwest during season (about $50 per trip), Vail at Thanksgiving, at least two additional Colorado trips, and a ten-day European jaunt. You must be 21 to join. For details and date of next meeting, write Box A, 1455 Sandburg Village, Chicago 60610. Dues $18 first year, $8 thereafter.

Windy City Grotto. Chicago chapter of National Speleological Society devoted to poking into and exploring caves. Interracial. Mainly college to early 30s; men outnumber women three to one. Winter meetings are small—maybe only 40 members—ideal for making friends. Meet second Wednesday, 7:30 PM, at Field Museum (guard will let you in) for programs of slides, films, lectures, and discussions. Field trips to southern Indiana and Missouri caves. Dues $3. Show up at museum or contact Bill Mixon, editor, *Windy City Speleo News*, 5035N S. Drexel, 924-0441.

Chicago Mountaineering Club. Another organization in which men outnumber women three to one. Meets second Thursday, 8 PM, at Field Museum. Offers at least 15 weekend climbs yearly—to Starved Rock State Park, Ill., in winter for ice climbing; to Mississippi Palisades State Park, Ill., for limestone cliffs and pinnacles; and to the club campsite at Devil's Lake, Wis., where quartzite cliffs of splendid quality present different climbing problems. Novices welcome—you'll learn how to climb safely in rope teams. Transportation on a share-a-ride basis if you haven't a car. Outings are inexpensive—you sleep in tents at Devil's Lake. To join, be 18 or older, attend three outings, get endorsement from two members. Initiation fee $10. Dues $8, nonresident (more than 100 miles away) $5. Contact George Griffin, 105 Flagstaff Lane, Hoffman Estates 60172.

Sierra Club (p. 134-135) is highly outing-oriented—don't overlook.

Chicago Archaeological Society. Interracial society of professionals and lay people offers lectures by archaeologists and anthropologists, takes field trips to areas of archaeological activity in Illinois, does survey work, and occasionally helps at digs. Goals are scholarly—like discouraging trafficking in artifacts. Membership of 150 is wonderfully diverse. Meets last Sunday of month, 7:30 PM, for coffee and conversation, 8 PM lecture at Chicago Academy of Sciences, 2001 N. Clark. Membership $9 single, $4 student, $13 family. Contact Stanley Stec, 916 Prairie, Des Plaines, AR 1-0482 after 6 PM.

Chicago Chess Club, 10 N. LaSalle, 372-0700. Oldest and largest chess club in Midwest, founded 1870. A good place to meet serious chess players. Integrated membership of 340—one-third high school and college students, almost all the rest ages 20-45. Potential members welcome two-three times, then asked to decide about joining. Dues $50 adult men; $35 college students, women, and members living outside 50-mile radius; $25 high school students. Facilities for 80 players. Continuous Rapid Transit and Swiss System Tournaments. Monday chess instruction with masters, 7-10 PM; $2 member, $4 nonmember. Sets are Standard Staunton Tournament sets and old German wood sets with four-inch kings. Open noon-midnight daily. Club can also inform you of all tournaments in Chicago area.

Oak Park Chess Club, Carroll Center, Kenilworth & Filmore, Oak Park. Fine mix of chess people here. All ages, both sexes, married, widowed, divorced. Serious chess every Tuesday 7-10 PM, yet for a game that's considered one of the two most aggressive, players surprise with their gentleness. Nice park district facility—a pretty, rustic, well-lighted, little building in the middle of a park. Occasional voluntary dues to buy more equipment. Club is member of U.S. Chess Federation, sanctioned for rated tournaments. Free instruction available, but knowledge of basics essential. Oak Park residency not required. Contact Tony Licata evenings, weekends, 848-2578.

Civil War Round Table. Men only in this serious-interest group steeped in the long-dead armies, battles, causes, events of the Civil War. Monthly dinner meeting with speaker (member or imported expert) at Chicago Bar Assn., second Friday each month. Annual battlefield tour in spring. Dues $20, include subscription to the quarterly journal *Civil War History.* Contact Abraham Lincoln Book Shop, 18 E. Chestnut, WH 4-3085.

The Westerners, Chicago Corral. The one requirement for membership is a passion for the factual history of the American West. Dinner conversation at the monthly meeting may be mainly banter, but the paper that follows is always meaty, covers an aspect of frontier history, such as the legends, the humor, the songs, the men and women who settled the West. About 34-40 members of all ages show up at each meeting. Though no women have yet asked to join, they're welcome. Regular membership $20, corresponding nonresident $8, reduced dues for students. Dinner (in a restaurant or club) about $6. Guests welcome; it's assumed if you show up twice, you'll want to join. Contact Sheriff Alvin Krieg, 210 E. Pearson, SU 7-1412.

Baker Street Irregulars. Chicago chapter (Hugo's Companions) is just as Sherlock Holmes-oriented as any chapter but more staunchly all male than many. Meets Sept.-July at Baker Street Pub, Hartford Plaza Bldg., 365 W. Monroe. Dinners, discussion, papers, quizzes in the best literary society tradition. Also occasional featured speakers. Dues $10, include subscription to *Baker Street Journal.* Write Robert Hahn, president, at the pub (zip: 60606).

Dickens Fellowship. Your membership card comes from headquarters in London and includes privileges for special Dickensian events in England. This group (small—about 30-40 members) is one of 60 chapters around the world. Members here are in their 50s and 60s, mostly married but some widowers. Meet two-three times yearly for dramatic or humorous reading or a skit on the Victorian age. Also annual Christmas party plus joint meetings with Friends of Literature in fall and spring. Dues $3.50, include subscription to *Dickensian* magazine, published in London. Contact Jesse Morton, 803 S. Chester, Park Ridge, 698-3577.

Friends of Literature. Much larger membership than Dickens Fellowship but in same age bracket. October-April program of monthly luncheon or dinner meetings followed by guest speakers. Dues $7.50. Contact Mrs. Hazel R. Ferguson, 1500 Chicago, Evanston, 475-6107.

Young Friends of the Arts, 22 W. Monroe, 263-3314. A nonprofit, student-run organization for high school, college, part-time, and graduate students. Gets half-priced or reduced-rate tickets to major concerts, recitals, plays, musicals, cabaret theatre, ballet and dance series and free admission to museums, film previews, special events. Brings you together with others through meetings, forums, steering council, social events. Serves as clearing house for summer jobs in the arts. Membership $5.

Museum of Contemporary Art Affiliates, Museum of Contemporary Art, 237 E. Ontario, 943-7755. Four affiliate groups here: Near North Side, South Side, North Shore, Fox River Valley. Each group does its own thing—backstage tours, open rehearsals of Chicago Symphony Orchestra, lecture tours of private art collections, recitals, whatever. At least half the activities are scheduled for young wives who have free time on weekdays. Membership $5 plus membership in the museum ($15).

Chicago School of Architecture Foundation, 1800 S. Prairie (Glessner House), 326-1393. Architects and buffs join this foundation to socialize with others who realize that architecture is more than buildings. Programs include lectures and stylish exhibition openings which always bring out the city's leading architects. Docent program, a selective, high-power free course, teaches you to conduct tours of Chicago's great architecture. At least one-third of membership is single; average age mid-30s. Membership $15, student $5.

Nautical Research & Model Ship Society of Chicago. Serious research society interested in naval architecture and detail and authenticity of historical materials. Works with admiralties in Great Britain, Scandinavia, and elsewhere; provides services, such as verification of documents, to maritime museums. Members build models of extraordinary craftsmanship (plank-on-frame construction, for instance) and superb detailing—the antithesis of building from ship-model kits. All-male membership simply because women generally aren't interested in lengthy discussions about rigs on 18th-century brigantines or the proper woods for models. Meets second Saturday, Illinois Room, YMCA Hotel, 826 S. Wabash. Ages 20s-70s. Dues $7.50. Contact D.L. McCalip, secretary, 5658 S. Hermitage, 436-2109.

Chicago Horticultural Society, 18 S. Michigan, DE 2-2868. Membership includes lectures, box-lunch workshops, and demonstrations at Botanic Garden (the Society supports it); tours to outstanding Midwest public and private gardens and commercial growing centers; notable horticultural events; discounts at the Society's plant sales; subscription to *Garden Talk;* use of the Society's extensive library. Board is strongly Old Guard North Shore, but membership (2,100) is beginning to broaden. For instance, all members of Chicago's West Chesterfield Garden Club are black. The Society is also an umbrella organization for 17 specialized plant societies in the area, can direct you to Daylily, Rose, Midwest Bonsai, or whatever you might wish to join. Tax-deductible dues $15.

Earth Science Club of Northern Illinois. Family-oriented club holds formal programs in Downers Grove and goes on field trips to enhance knowledge of archaeology, paleontology, micromount (crystal form), and geology. For information, Lizzadro Museum of Lapidary Art, 220 Cottage Hill (Wilder Park), Elmhurst, 833-1616. Dues $2 single, $3.25 couple, 75¢ under 16.

Chicago Rocks & Minerals Society. Another good group for families. Meets at Green Briar Field House, 2650 W. Peterson, RO 4-3008, 8:30 PM, second

Saturday. Programs include annual auction, field trips, and study groups in mineral identification, fossils, geology. Dues $3 adult, $1 junior.

Gold Coast Kennel Club, 64 W. Ohio, 664-4664. For dog owners (any kind of dog) who have a sense of responsibility about dog ownership. Meets monthly, 7:45 PM, at St. Regis Hotel, 516 N. Clark, for lectures, films, discussions. Offers reliable help with care, training, grooming, purchasing, breeding, traveling with dog. Acknowledges ecology problem, is trying for viable accommodation between urban dog owners and dog haters, and among many goals wants to set up permanent outdoor exercise areas. Membership includes veterinarians and lawyers. Dues $20 individual, $5 each additional member of family.

Chicago Ornithological Society. Nonprofessional bird-watching club meets second Wednesday, 7 PM, at Field Museum for programs of slides, films, speakers, reports of new birds observed, etc. Sunday field trips once or twice each month plus occasional overnighters to Horicon Marsh, Wis., or Jasper-Pulaski State Park, Ind. One scientific venture yearly not open to rank amateurs: the Christmas Bird Watch, sponsored by Audubon Society, in which all birds within a 15-mile circle are counted in ten hours—a grand way to spend Christmas Eve or New Year's Day. Membership of 150, predominantly ages 40-60. Would happily be interracial if blacks wanted to join. Dues $3. Contact Peter Dring, Little Red School House Nature Center, TE 9-6897, or simply show up at a meeting.

Evanston Bird Club (energetic members, ages 35-45) meets at Evanston Public Library. **Lake-Cook Chapter of Illinois Audubon Society** meets in Highland Park at Trinity Episcopal Church (mostly couples, occasional family outings). Bird-watching societies abound in the suburbs. For other groups, write Illinois Audubon Society, 1017 Burlington, Downers Grove 60515. For Chicago Audubon, see p. 135.

Lively Church Groups. Almost every church and temple in Chicago and the suburbs sponsors or shelters a singles group. The trick with church groups is to shop around until you find one that meets at least some of your needs. Don't worry about religious affiliation—this is the age of ecumenism. Here are two, for instance, that couldn't care less what your religion is.

Near North Unitarian-Universalist Fellowship, 1755 N. North Park. Contact John and Linda LaPlante, 2522 W. Winnemac, 728-0386. Liberal organization with large group called Singulars creates activities on a kind of consensus basis—if ten people are interested in a new idea (potluck suppers, for instance, or gestalt encounter groups), a subgroup forms. Singles, mainly late 20s-early 30s, as many men as women. Fellowship members to mid-50s.

Unitarian Singles, First Unitarian Church, 5650 S. Woodlawn, FA 4-4100. Alert organization, mid-20s to early 50s, mainly divorced. Programs include lectures, discussion groups, entertainment, always preceded and followed by social hour.

Square Dancing. Find 100-150 different groups in Chicago and suburbs. Caller Marvin Labahn, 10853 S. Parkside, Chicago Ridge 60415, will direct you to those in your area. He'll also supply *Square Facts*, a quarterly directory of square-, round-, or folk-dance groups. Phone 423-9222 after 6 PM.

Folk Dancing. Ethnic dancing, sometimes between couples but just as often in trios, a line, or small circles. Contact Frank and Dee Alsberg, 1827 W. Pratt, 973-2860, for information on all groups.

Geja Wine Society meets quarterly at Geja's Cafe, 340 W. Armitage, 281-9101, for wine-tasting seminars and discussions with experts. Membership $5. About 150 members turn out for each seminar.

Chicagoland Sports Car Club. Primarily a racing club with about 180 members, mainly male. They drive hard, work on cars and at races on timing, scoring, or on tech inspection team. Meet fourth Wednesday, 8 PM, at Seven Oaks Restaurant, 7501 W. Roosevelt, Forest Park; everyone goes out for drinks afterward. Two members must sponsor you, but it's easy—just show up at meetings and be friendly. Write P.O. Box 224, Evanston 60204, or check ads in foreign car section of Sunday papers.

PURELY SOCIAL

Singles Bars. Make up your mind about these. If you enjoy them, you have a head start. If you don't like them, why keep going?

Except for Playboy Towers, which is mass-scene Playboy Atmosphere, and The Bull and Bear, which is highly interracial, singles bars scarcely differentiate themselves. They all have "specials"—two drinks for the price of one during weekday cocktail hours, freebie 5¢ food (a hot dog, a piece of chicken, chili) on weekend afternoons. Friday is always the biggest night, followed by Wednesday and Saturday in that order.

Santa Claus Anonymous is one group every newcomer to the Near North Side wants to join. It's a mob of swingers that hold exactly two pay-admission, cash-bar parties—one in December and another in May—to raise money for 600 needy children in Chicago public schools. Contact Michael Tighe, Jr., Northern Trust, 346-5500.

Laundromats are excellent meeting grounds. If you're male, ask the female at the next machine for advice on bleach; if you're female, your quarter's stuck. Time is on your side in the coin-op; you can't possibly wash and dry a load in much less than an hour, and the setup is far more subtle than any singles bar.

Computer Dating. Forget it. Filling out a computer date form in which you describe yourself is overkill. On a form, you'll do your best to make yourself sound as attractive as possible. So does everyone else.

T-groups, encounter groups, sensitivity groups probably have as much to do with meeting people as with anything else, but don't join with the hope of finding someone with whom to develop a significant relationship. People with problems get involved in these groups, and that's the drawback. Troubled people are egocentric; until an egocentric solves his problems, his interests are almost totally in himself.

One possible exception: **Oasis, Midwest Center for Human Potential,** 20 E. Harrison, 922-5964. Although it offers encounter and gestalt groups, transactional analysis, and encounter marathons, it emphasizes a focus on self-awareness in its literature, says that its workshops and programs are not offered as cures for emotional problems. Sunday evening open encounter drop-in for singles and couples might be worth investigating—depends on what you're looking for. Four-hour session begins at 6:30 PM. Admission $4, $2 for students.

BEING CREATIVE

Creative groups abound. Community theatre, symphony orchestras, and choral societies enrich an astonishing number of suburbs. Dance groups, arts and crafts classes, photography clubs are proliferating. Some of the most professional with the highest standards are described here. To learn of others, phone **Illinois Arts Council,** 111 N. Wabash, 793-3520. The council is a first-rate source of current information about performing arts groups, can tell you who to contact where, also knows of art centers and film-making groups. Or contact your local chamber of commerce or welcome wagon.

Community Theatre. Expect to give it all your free time because professionalism counts—at least with the theatres listed below. One or two Equity actors are often in casts; the theatres in turn occasionally produce Equity performers. Since community theatre is volunteer, you can also be part of the group by offering to do production work—tech help, stage design, costume, publicity, box office. Shop around.* Each theatre has its own schtick. Open casting unless otherwise noted. Interracial for the most part. Workshops affiliated with most.

Kingston Mines, 2356 N. Lincoln, 525-9893. Specializes in experimental American drama which it performs with original manuscripts, avant-garde techniques. Emphasizes communication above content. Theatre seats 300 on bleachers in big space. June Pyskacek, director.

Old Town Players, 1718 N. North Park, 645-0145. Performs in a wonderfully intimate little theatre. Does revivals of substance—Ibsen, Henry James, Pirandello; occasionally strays into operetta. Very high standards. Frank Carioti, director.

New Chicago City Players, 615 W. Wellington, 929-0542. Humanistic theatre uses approaches of humanistic psychology to explore and heighten onstage action. Tries to extend audience self-image through drama. Works continuously with videotape. Some scripts, but emphasis is on improvisation. Ted Sarantos, director.

Kuumba Workshop, P.O. Box 17368, Chicago 60617, 374-3240. Takes its name from the African word "kuumba" (to create). Performances are rituals, not plays, since part of the workshop's mission is to break from Western theatre tradition. Kuumba believes black art comes directly from and must reflect black life—hence, chants, hymns, street idiom, the words of black artists are given form to make them recognizable as art. Gives at least one ritual each weekend at South Side Community Art Center, 3831 S. Michigan. Val Gray Ward, director.

---

* Check "Front Row Center" in "Two" section of *Chicago Sun-Times* for casting notices.

Jane Addams Theatre, 3212 N. Broadway, 549-1631. Does small intimate drama (*The Physicists* and *Slow Dance on the Killing Ground*) and one-background comedies. Proceeds help support various Hull House community centers. This theatre is located in one. Directors vary.

Free Theater, 3257 N. Sheffield, 929-6920. Specializes in rock cantata and rock opera with splendid lighting effects and music. Uses singers, dancers, band instrumentalists. Usual way to performing role is by joining company class (meets one night per week, teaches free theory, some movement; $25 per semester). Also room for volunteers as tech people, door watchers, what-have-you. William Russo, director.

North Shore Theatre Company. Affiliate of Wilmette Recreation Board, AL 1-9505. Very fine, well-established group, more classical than most; in recent seasons did *Merchant of Venice, Dark of the Moon, Fiddler on the Roof.* Attracts people with good acting backgrounds or professional aspirations from as far as Waukegan and Hyde Park. Pays established directors and tech directors.

Chicago Park District, 294-2320, sponsors productions and free drama classes in multiple locations. Park District views the effort mainly as recreational theatre, but there are exceptions, especially at LaFollette, Loyola, Margate, Ridge, and Lincoln Park. This last is the Park District's special art theatre; it has open casting, but for certain plays or lead roles the director works from a preferred list.

Poetry Workshop. Columbia College Center for New Music, 3257 N. Sheffield. Attracts large weekly crowds of hopeful poets on Thursdays, 8:30 PM, from Sept. to July. Show up to read your own poetry, get a critique, have it reproduced underground.

Instrumental Music Groups. Far more groups perform or play for the joy of it than can possibly be listed below. Orchestras here are simply some of the best known with the most professional standards. Inquire if you feel you're qualified. If you're not, somebody helpful will guide you to a group you'll enjoy. Dues average $10 yearly for music and rehearsal hall.

DePaul University Community Symphony Orchestra, 25 E. Jackson, WE 9-3525. Qualified instrumentalists are invited to audition each September. Performances always include three concerts at Orchestra Hall. Leon Stein, dean of the music school, directs.

Chicago Business Men's Orchestra. A fully instrumented orchestra of above-average amateurs and top students who want symphonic training. Performances include concerts at the Auditorium. Contact Lester R. Baker, business manager, 1207 Helen Court, Ingleside, 587-5277.

Civic Orchestra of Chicago, Orchestra Hall, 427-7711. Auditions young (to 29) musicians—all instruments—each spring for soloist performances. The Civic is the training orchestra for the Chicago Symphony Orchestra. Conductors vary. Gordon Peters, administrator.

North Side Symphony Orchestra. A true community enterprise that performs seven concerts yearly, with final concert at Orchestra Hall. About 80-100 instrumentalists ages 14-71. Rehearsals at Paul Revere Park Field House Friday evenings, Sept.-June. Show up, or contact conductor, Milton Preves, principal violist of Chicago Symphony Orchestra, at his home, 724-0855.

Evanston Symphony Orchestra. A fine, full symphony orchestra directed by Frank Miller, principal cellist of Chicago Symphony Orchestra. Performs five-six times Sept.-May, rehearses Tuesdays, 7:30 PM, at Evanston Township High School. Not limited to Evanstonians. For audition information, contact Sam Gordon, 728-0095.

Other symphony orchestras to investigate: Community Music Assn./Lake Forest Symphony; Skokie Valley Symphony Orchestra; Du Page Symphony Orchestra; Northwest Symphony Orchestra (Des Plaines); Southwest Symphony Orchestra (Oak Lawn); Chicago Heights Symphony Orchestra; Elgin Symphony Orchestra.

North Shore Concert Band, sponsored by Wilmette Recreation Board, AL 1-9505. Concertizes at Gilson Park Bowl, Wilmette, in summer and in high school auditoriums in winter. Travels in and out of state to give fund-raising performances. Weekly rehearsals year-round. Works from tremendous library of classical music. John Paynter, director of Northwestern University bands, conducts.

Amateur Chamber Music Players, Inc. Membership of 5,000 across the U.S. includes more than 200 members in Chicago and suburbs. Annual directory lists names, phone numbers, addresses, instruments played by each member, plus each member's evaluation of his own performance level— excellent, good, fair, pro. Members also compose and circulate new chamber music, feel free to call one another to play together here and in other cities when traveling. For current directory and details, write Miss Helen Rice, secretary, ACMP, 15 W. 67th, New York, N.Y. 10023. No fee, but members contribute a few dollars each year to cover mailings, newsletter, etc.

American Recorder Society, Chicago Chapter. Plays for personal enjoyment at all levels, though if you've studied piano ten years and theory five, you'll be frustrated. For everyone else, it's the place to meet the nicest group of people and play recorder at the same time. Mainly age 25 up. Informal sessions Sunday, 2-5 PM, St. James Cathedral, 65 E. Huron. Contact Mrs. Donald Austin, 112 S. Clinton, Oak Park 60302, 386-1580.

Joal Fischer, producer of Chicago Masquers, is the man to call if you want to play Renaissance instruments with other musicians. He can help you find or organize the right group. Phone 866-6290.

Old Town School of Folk Music, 909 W. Armitage, 525-7472. Atmosphere is relaxed, informal, and highly conducive to meeting others because a group feeling is deliberately created through coffee breaks and sing-alongs. Classes for beginners through advanced levels in guitar, banjo, mountain dulcimer, classical guitar, harmonica. Sit in once or twice as a visitor, borrow an instrument to see if you really want to learn it.

Performing Vocal Groups. These range from the total professionalism of the Chicago Symphony Chorus to church choirs that sing more than the Sunday services. Also check the bulletin boards at Carl Fischer's music store, 312 S. Wabash; all sorts of musical groups looking for more singers post notices here.

Chicago Symphony Chorus, Orchestra Hall, 427-7711. Auditions one or more times yearly for all voice parts in its superb chorus. Essential to be first-rate because half of chorus is professional. You need a background in music theory, repertoire, sight reading. Audition requirements include one song in foreign language and one in English. Performances throughout year with the Chicago Symphony Orchestra. Margaret Hillis, director.

Grant Park Symphony Chorus. Auditions singers in all categories Feb.-March for upcoming summer season. Audition requires one aria in a foreign language, one in English. Excellent training under Thomas Peck, director. Phone Grant Park Concert Office, 294-2420, for details.

Lyric Opera Chorus. Main auditions in Feb., rehearses March-Sept. All voice categories in regular choral complement and auxiliary group. Positions are professional under terms of American Guild of Musical Artists contracts. Michael Lepore, chorus master. For details, Lyric Opera, FI 6-6111.

To be a spear bearer or other super for Lyric, call first or second week in September, ask to speak to whoever's in charge of supers. Get token payment, $2, for each rehearsal and performance. Expect more rehearsals here than in other opera companies, more chance to be around principal singers. Most rehearsals weekends and evenings but not all—you may have to take off a couple of hours from work once or twice.

Savoy-Aires. Performs Gilbert & Sullivan on North Shore. Welcomes G&S buffs, singers, anyone else interested in joining the group in any capacity, especially production. The ubiquitous Frank Miller of the Chicago Symphony Orchestra is musical director; members of the Evanston Symphony Orchestra are his pit men. Rehearsals in summer in Evanston churches. Mrs. Robert Circle, producer, 272-3072.

Note: Gilbert & Sullivan Opera Company on the South Side does one fat production each winter at Mandel Hall on University of Chicago campus. It's a university community group that makes sense to join if you're living in the area. Roland Bailey, musical director, 947-5741 weekdays, 324-0420 after 6 PM.

Chicago Chamber Choir. A choral society that specializes in rarely heard choral literature, especially medieval music, and performs very ambitious programs. Rehearsals Tuesday evenings at Church of Our Savior, 530 W. Fullerton. George T. Estevez, director, GR 2-0555.

Niles Concert Choir, Niles College, 7135 N. Harlem, 823-1056. Excellent choral group that performs several times yearly, at least once each season with full symphony orchestra in Orchestra Hall. Tackles big music—Beethoven's *Missa Solemnis,* Verdi's *Requiem;* presented Midwest premieres of Bernstein's *Chichester Psalms* and Britten's *War Requiem.* Rev. Stanley Rudcki, director.

Apollo Musical Club, 243 S. Wabash, HA 7-5620. Enormous (200 members) old oratorio society that just celebrated its centennial. Auditions Sept.-Oct. and Jan.-March following Monday night rehearsals at YMCA Hotel, 826 S. Wabash. Ages 17 through 80, fully interracial. Performs at least three concerts in Loop yearly, including annual *Messiah* at Orchestra Hall. Dues $20 per season. Conductor William J. Peterman is also director of performing arts, New Trier High School.

Music Theatre of Hyde Park. Musicals only—*Kiss Me Kate, Fiorello, Guys & Dolls, How To Succeed in Business, Once upon a Mattress, Pal Joey.* Excellent training ground. Open auditions for vocalists, instrumentalists; can always use set designers and production personnel. Ages 16 to mid-50s, interracial. Performs at excellent Beverly Art Center Theatre. Janice (Mrs. Arthur) Roberts, director; Arthur Roberts, music director, 1 S 176 Rochdale, Lombard 60148, 629-2646.

Art Classes. If you're good enough and can carry it off, paint on a large canvas in a conspicuous high-traffic spot in a park. You'll meet people. Otherwise, take art instruction. The range of instruction in Chicago is highly varied. People attending night classes at the Art Institute or the Evanston Art Center are generally wholly serious about their work, but it's not hard to find classes where you can enjoy the socializing as much as the creative effort.

Art Institute of Chicago, Adams & Michigan, CE 6-7080. Phone for evening school brochure. Superb classes in all aspects of the fine arts under a prestigious staff.

Contemporary Art Workshop, 542 W. Grant, LA 5-9624. Serious and advanced work under artists of national repute, especially Cosmo Campoli (sculpture, carving, casting in plaster, stone, wood, clay); John Kearney (metal sculpture, wax, welding); Paul Zakoian (sculpture in wood, clay, stone). Painting classes by workshop associates who rent studios here. Small classes, never more than 15.

Old Town Triangle Center, 1818 N. Wells, MI 2-4262. Art classes in wide variety of subjects, including photography and collage. Also Saturday outdoor sketching. Staff consists of well-known area artists, some also on Art Institute staff.

Printmakers' Studio, 3335 N. Halsted, 477-5959. Relief printing (woodcut, found object, embossing, texture experimenting, color, fabric). Also silk screening and etching—drypoint, line etch, aquatint, soft ground, sugar lift, chine collé, viscosity printing. If you know printmaking techniques and want to use the workshop facilities, ask about the associate program. Gustav Pausz and Steve Lumpkin direct studio.

414 Art Workshop, 414 N. State, 944-8329. A variety of arts and crafts classes here. Gretchen Rogers teaches one of the best—sketch classes applicable to layout and fashion illustration—a warm group experience shared by people of all ages. Shirley Walters directs the entire operation.

Also worth investigating:

Hyde Park Art Center, 5236 S. Blackstone, 363-9565
Beverly Art Center, 2153 W. 111th, 445-3838
Bernard Horwich Jewish Community Center, 3003 W. Touhy, RO 1-9100
South Side Community Art Center, 3831 S. Michigan, DR 3-8666
Oak Park Art League, 720 Chicago, Oak Park, 386-9853
Evanston Art Center, 2603 Sheridan Rd., Evanston, GR 5-5300
North Shore Art League, 620 Lincoln, Winnetka, HI 6-2870
Suburban Fine Arts Center, 472 Park, Highland Park, 432-1888
Libertyville Art Center, 1700 N. Milwaukee, Libertyville, EM 2-0707
Park Forest Art Center, 400 Lakewood, Park Forest, 748-3377

Note: Most art centers also offer crafts classes.

Photography. Nobody knows the total number of photography clubs in the Chicago area, but at least 60 clubs make up the **CACCA (Chicago Area Camera Club Assn.).** Contact Wilbur Jensen, 3110 W. 114th Pl., FU 8-0696, for club in your area.

Fort Dearborn Camera Club, 220 S. State, 939-9561. One of CACCA's most prestigious clubs, with seven darkrooms, studio facilities, evening school of photography, field trips, Friday meetings, and bimonthly photo competitions. It's a great place to meet people; members help each other and direct you to still other members who'll come in to work with you, sharing specific areas of expertise. More men than women. Interracial. Call or write for application and interview for membership. Initiation fee $25. Monthly dues $5 single, $7.50 couple. Darkroom fee $2.

Crafts

The Clay People, 3345 N. Halsted, 528-5156. Classes in handmade stoneware for beginners and experienced potters. Attracts an interesting people mix from a Playboy secretary to an army colonel. Also a separate firing service (bisque-cone 08 and glaze-cone 9 reduction) for anyone who works with clay but does not have a kiln. Contact Bruce or Marsha Jacobson.

Weaving Workshop, 3324 N. Halsted, 929-5776. Barbara Pleason-di Mauro teaches four-harness weaving, rug weaving, tapestry techniques, fabric design, patterns on loom—even how to spin wool and build a loom.

American Craftsman, 2348½ N. Clark, 929-1080. Varied craft classes under excellent instructors: weaving (make your own loom first), batik dyeing, macrame, quilting, and the like. For stitching lessons, **Nimble Needles,** at same address, 327-3460.

Nina Needlepoint, 120 E. Delaware, 642-7066. Small-group lessons (four or five people) in one of the few needlepoint places that attract men as well as women.

Needlemania, 66 E. Walton, 664-3511. Lots of socializing with customers giving each other pointers. Young men also feel comfortable here.

CHAPTER IX

MAKING NEW FRIENDS—METHOD B

Method B for making friends gets you involved in groups with goals. The goals may be primarily self-interest, as in Divorce Anonymous. Or they may be as basic to the national interest as those of the American Civil Liberties Union. Or they may be focused on specific issues, as in the National Organization for Women.

Through legitimate political action, you can help bring about changes you believe in—and at the same time meet others who feel the same way. In other words, it's your country, your environment, your city, your people— and if you don't like what's happening to these, you can, through group effort, do something worthwhile. And not be lonely.

POLITICAL ACTION & SOCIAL CHANGE

Political action in the 1970s is people making their voices heard through group effort and using the political process to create change. Being a member of one of these groups can be a powerful experience.

Independent Precinct Organization, 940 W. Belmont, 248-3886. Here's a group with several goals. IPO is a political-action organization that works not merely before elections but year-round on issues and for political reform.

IPO believes that the institutions of a community must be responsive to the community and that people in office (or candidates for office) should be supported because of their value to the community rather than because of their party loyalty.

If you're interested in what happens to Chicago, this is a first-rate group to join.

Chapters, organized in the following wards, meet regularly: 1st, 2nd, 32nd, 34th, 35th, 40th, 42nd, 43rd, 44th, 46th, 47th, 48th, 49th, 50th. Chapters also are great dating organizations. Dues: $1 up—whatever you wish to contribute. Requisite for membership: you guarantee to work actively during elections.

Independent Voters of Illinois, 22 W. Monroe, 263-4274. Bipartisan organization lobbying occasionally in Springfield and endorsing candidates at elections. Year-round program of consumer advocacy and watchdog exposure. For instance, IVI recently exposed a huge number of fraudulent signatures on the nominating petition of a regular Democratic organization candidate and uncovered a militant right-wing group accused of using terror tactics. IVI is the Illinois affiliate of Americans for Democratic Action. Dues $12.50 single, $15 family, $3 student.

American Civil Liberties Union, 6 S. Clark, 726-6180. ACLU is dedicated to protecting civil liberties as it sees them—hence takes as legal cases only those it regards as significant and precedent setting. Also lobbies for legislation and is active in political campaigns. Joining is a way of participating in the defense of everyone's Constitutional rights. How actively you get involved in headquarters work depends on your skills. Dues $10 single, $15 family, $5 limited income or student.

Committee on Illinois Government, 33 N. Dearborn, RA 6-9646. Main thrust: excellence in government at state and local levels. Helps interested citizens affect legislation in Springfield and Chicago City Council. Keeps you current on pending bills, shows how to bring about their passage or defeat. Also can help other issue-oriented groups double their effectiveness, get sponsorship of new bills, etc. Monthly luncheon with speakers plus immediate committee work of your choice. Dues $15.

League of Women Voters, 67 E. Madison, CE 6-0315. Basis of League efforts is self-education via workshops, public information (especially at elections), and honest elections. Goal is an informed electorate, starting with League members. Also watchdogs issues—welfare, health, education, pollution. Lobbies when state legislature is in session. Almost every woman in politics started with the League. Dues $10.

National Organization for Women, 922-0025. NOW believes in change through peaceful legal channels. Chicago chapter does most of its work in committees: Direct Action, Education, Abortion Repeal, Image of Women in Media, Public Relations, Employment, Legal, Child Care. You'll be urged to become active in one or several.

Women's Liberation Center of Evanston, at Wheadon Methodist Church, 2214 Ridge, Evanston, 475-4480.

Medical Committee for Human Rights, 2251 W. Taylor, 243-4137. National organization growing by leaps (45 new chapters added last year), gets you deeply involved in health care issues. As these bump against every aspect of society, MCHR is into housing, drugs, pollution, free clinics in communities that have no health services, school lunch programs, occupational health problems, health services for prisoners, and mental health. Activist in best sense of the word. All work done in task forces; you're expected to do research to understand problems you work on. Members are primarily physicians, RNs, med students, psychiatric social workers; but MCHR welcomes concerned lay people, especially needs volunteer typists and people with communicative skills. Dues structured to income, from $5 student fee up, waived when necessary.

Co-Ordinating Council for Handicapped Children, 407 S. Dearborn, 939-3513. Volunteer coalition of 200 members plus 36 member organizations of concerned parents and professionals. Goal: to get for approximately 100,000 handicapped* Chicago children all benefits other children get as a matter of course. Sturdily activist, the Council helps parents organize effective parent groups (Parent Power); meets monthly; conducts special workshops; marches when essential; holds rallies and press conferences to get legislative action;

---

* Handicapped child is defined as any child whose emotional, mental, or physical condition requires a special service. Less than half of all handicapped Chicago children are presently getting the services they're entitled to.

knows exactly what's going on at any time in state legislature and Congress. Advice in its 92-page booklet, *How To Organize an Effective Parent Group & Move Bureaucracies,* will work for any group trying to get off the ground ($1.50 plus 10¢ postage). Dues $5.

Operation PUSH (People United To Save Humanity), 930 E. 50th, 373-3366, or P.O. Box 5432, Chicago 60680. National organization dedicated to securing justice for all people by challenging those economic, political, and social forces that make some human beings—black, poor, aged, all those in need—subservient to others. Weekly Saturday morning meetings (8:30 AM-noon) are both religious services and urban affairs meetings on matters that affect black community. Rev. Jesse L. Jackson speaks at 10 AM. Most work done in divisions, such as Political Education, Teachers, Health, Youth, Direct Action. To join, buy a PUSH card ($3 up—any amount you wish to pay). The card enables you to attend all meetings and work on a committee. Interracial but predominantly black.

Urban League, 4500 S. Michigan, AT 5-5800. Main thrust: improvement of race relations through negotiation, community education, and community organization. Also acts as a referral agency for people who need legal aid, housing, health services, family counseling. If you're really committed, you may, after training, participate in volunteer speakers' bureau, do research (all action is based on research), or work in housing, education, employment, health, welfare. Board is biracial; membership predominantly black. Membership contribution $1 or as much more as you wish.

Citizens Action Program, 600 W. Fullerton, 929-2922. One of the biggest (4,000 members) activist groups in the city. CAP tackles major city problems: pollution, inequitable real estate taxes, and the Board of Education's wasteful spending habits. In the case of the Crosstown Expressway, which it says will displace 10,000 Chicagoans, it also takes on City Hall. Based on earlier successful experience against Commonwealth Edison (emissions), it knows how to lobby, how to confront local pols, how to get press attention. Go to meetings as member or not; learn what's been done, what you can do. CAP is idea-oriented; your ideas will be welcomed. Join nearest chapter, and get on one of its committees. Pay dues if you can: $3 student, $5 adult.

MetroCenter. A new group of singles creates its own volunteer social-action programs. Lots of room here to research and activate ideas you've always believed were needed but couldn't get off the ground by yourself. Members mainly ages 25-35 from city and suburbs. Membership $12, but won't turn you down if you can't afford to pay. Contact through Lawson YMCA, 30 W. Chicago, 944-6211.

Mattachine Midwest, 4753 N. Broadway, 334-2244. Anyone 18 years or older, regardless of sex or sexual orientation, can join—under pseudonym if you wish. Active program seeks to improve the legal, social, and economic status of homosexuals. Also can refer you to physicians, lawyers, psychologists, employment counselors, draft advisers, and clergymen on 24-hour basis. Dues $5 for half year.

Chicago Gay Alliance, 171 W. Elm, 664-4708. Double-purpose organization trying to change society's attitudes and help homosexuals achieve a healthier outlook about their homosexuality. Members mainly early 20s; majority are men, but more women join all the time. Regular attendance and committee work required. Social activities include dinners, receptions for authors. Dues $1 quarterly.

Divorce Anonymous, P.O. Box 5313, Chicago 60680, DI 2-9325. Not a social group but a way to get help from others who've been through the mill. Above all, a way to make friends when you need them most. DA really should be called Marriage & Divorce Anonymous because it can steer you to marriage and psychological counselors as well as to lawyers and social agencies. Program includes lectures, informal dinners in cafeterias and restaurants so you needn't eat alone, parties, and other group entertainment.

Parents Without Partners, P.O. Box 9255, Chicago 60690, 726-4429. Another self-help organization that tries to help you beat aloneness by providing new friends. Weekly meetings, with speakers, in city and suburbs. Socializing and Sunday parent-children activities. Also annual Father-with-Custody Forum. Answering service (24 hours) provides places and dates of upcoming events. Dues 75¢ weekly.

Young Single Parents. Prime goal: to offset loneliness. "You make friends here, you don't feel like a loser." Members fairly evenly divided between men and women. Men, mainly in sales, average age 29. Women, mainly secretaries, some nurses, some on aid, some getting support, average age 26. Three meetings each month feature speakers such as psychologists, the fourth reserved for open discussion. Also outside social activities, parties for children. Meet Wednesdays 8:30 PM at Francesco's Banquet Hall, 8465 W. Grand, River Grove. Membership $8 plus 75¢ each meeting you attend. Guests $1. Cash bar. Contact Tom Kraska, 795-7110.

Young Republicans. Active in some wards, nonexistent in others. YRs in the Near North Side's 42nd Ward are swinging singles, and some of their monthly meetings are purely social. They don't even care what your political affiliation is or what ward you live in—just join 'em. Average age 27. Good speakers when a meeting has political overtones. To locate executive officer of this or any other YRs, phone 793-3697.

Young Democrats exist only in wards where ward committeeman doesn't oppose them. Phone Democratic party office in your ward.

ECOLOGY & WILDLIFE GROUPS

Citizens for a Better Environment, 2561 N. Clark, 248-1984, and 109 S. Dearborn, 236-5670. Acts as a referral organization for a spectrum of conservation groups. Because it's impossible to list more than a few here, contact this organization to learn where to go to get involved.

Open Lands Project, 53 W. Jackson, 427-4256, also can refer you to organizations that will welcome you as a member.

Sierra Club, Great Lakes Chapter, 616 Delles Rd., Wheaton 60187, 665-3939. Unique organization because it doesn't simply fight to save the environment but helps members enjoy what they're trying to protect. Marvelous schedule of Midwest outings—one or more every weekend year-round: bicycling trips, backpacking trips, nature walks, bird-watching expeditions, canoe trips, rock climbing, spelunking, winter camp-outs, cross-country ski trips. Also, general meeting first Wednesday each month at Chicago Academy of Sciences, 2001 N. Clark, 7:30 PM. Annual dues $15 single, $22.50 couple, $5 junior member to age 14, $8 full-time student. One-time admission fee of $5 covers all members of immediate family joining at same time.

Chicago Audubon Society. New chapter of National Audubon, which tries to protect all wildlife and its habitats. Meetings, field trips, nature study at Audubon camps, special group travel opportunities. Dues $12 single, $15 family; includes subscription to Audubon magazine. Contact R. Sethuraman, 6414 N. Ridge, 262-1716.

Zero Population Growth, 100 E. Ohio, 644-0972. Chicago-area office can put you in touch with nearest of five chapters in the area. Prime goal: population stabilization through education in problems of overpopulation. Believes families should be limited to two children, that if more children are wanted, attempts should be made to adopt them. Zero maintains an active volunteer speakers' bureau. Dues $15, student $8.

Friends of the Earth. New Chicago chapter of international FOE deals with environmental problems. It's an active lobbying group pushing for passage of state conservation bills. Maintains a volunteer speakers' bureau and teaches conservation to children. Join through Friends of the Earth, 529 Commercial St., San Francisco, Calif. 94111, 415-391-4270. Annual dues $15, student $7.50. FOE, San Francisco, will notify this chapter, which will contact you. Local dues $3.

BEING A VOLUNTEER

Being a volunteer is a special way to meet people and often the best way for singles to find each other. Age is unimportant, race is unimportant, religion couldn't matter less.

Voluntary Action Center, Council for Community Services in Metropolitan Chicago, 64 E. Jackson, 427-9151. This is *the* clearinghouse for volunteers since it can match what you have to give to the needs of almost 400 agencies in Cook, Lake, and Du Page Counties. Because it's tuned in to every conceivable kind of project, it can steer you directly to the sort of work you want to do—and find it for you in an area that's not a geographical problem. If you have a work skill or interest it can't match, it will develop a program for you. Or it will train you for the kind of work you're interested in if you lack the necessary skills. VAC is sensitive and responsive to its volunteers. Except for a few other programs listed here (where it makes sense to apply directly), VAC is the place to begin.

Big Brothers of Metropolitan Chicago, 343 S. Dearborn, 427-0637. For men, single or married, who volunteer to befriend fatherless boys. You do not assume parental, legal, or financial responsibility for the boy assigned to you, but you accept the responsibility of becoming his friend. Your long-range goal is to give your boy a sense of security and be the kind of man he can identify with. Big Brothers is insight-oriented, knows that a fatherless boy needs to do things with a man. Expect to be carefully screened before you're matched to a boy.

Note: Mothers of fatherless sons are welcome to call this agency to register their sons for big brothers.

The Mother Bank, Children's Memorial Hospital, 2300 Children's Plaza, 649-4000. A program that wants mothers and grandmothers willing to take a good, tough training program and then give five days a week (six hours a day) for as many weeks as necessary to infants diagnosed as maternally deprived. You assume sole responsibility for bathing, feeding, rocking, playing with, and comforting one child. He'll need you two-four weeks, perhaps more. When he's discharged, you're expected to take a respite before starting with another child. Phone director of volunteers.

Volunteer Talent Pool, 620 Lincoln, Winnetka, 446-3302. A unique way of sharing what you know with youngsters in 22 suburban parochial and public schools. Volunteers serve as classroom aides to teachers, share their special knowledge about occupations, interests, hobbies with students in curriculum-related subjects. Age isn't important (volunteers can be as young as 17, as old as 80); interest in enriching classroom knowledge is. VTP serves four suburbs: Winnetka, Glencoe, Northfield, Kenilworth. Similar organizations called Volunteer Bureaus serve at least 20 additional suburbs and can be located through phone directories.

Foster Grandparent Program. A part-time employment program for senior citizens, 60-80, in which you work with handicapped children in hospitals and day care centers. Child handicaps can be emotional, physical, or both. You guarantee to work daily (four hours a day), in return get minimum hourly wage plus carfare and lunch. Pay is held to minimum wage so that it won't affect your social security benefits. Contact Mayor's Office for Senior Citizens, 223 N. Michigan, 744-7300.

Note: This office also has a new training program, **Extension for Services to Elderly Persons.** It wants retirees who'll enjoy working at community and tenant relations in senior citizen buildings; some lead programs or conduct classes for groups and clubs in those buildings.

Ward Offices of Independent Aldermen. The typical Chicago alderman shares a ward office with his ward committeeman. That office is usually open only a couple of times a week. Chicago's independent aldermen maintain their own ward offices, staff them with bright volunteers, keep them open on a Mon.-Sat. schedule with generous evening hours. If you live in an Independent's ward and want to be useful, volunteer at his ward office (it's often called something like "Citizens' Committee for . . ."). Find a choice of opportunities and the chance to assume any amount of responsibility you want. Work includes legislative research, report writing, constituent help (take complaints, follow through to city departments), general office work, and inventing and carrying out swinging fund-raising drives. These last are much fun and much work and also frequent because they're a way of keeping the ward offices open on a full-time-plus basis.

Independent aldermen and their offices are:

Ward	Alderman	Ward Office
5th	Leon Despres	1623 E. 55th, BU 8-7411
8th	William Cousins, Jr.	1910 E. 79th, 375-3377
15th	Fr. Francis Lawlor	1725 W. 69th, 778-1395
16th	Mrs. Anna Langford	1249 W. 63rd, 434-5535
40th	Seymour F. Simon	4844 N. Lincoln, 769-3074
43rd	William Singer	2258 N. Orchard, 281-1520
44th	Dick Simpson	1045 W. Belmont, 525-6034

Docent Program at The Oriental Institute, 1155 E. 58th, 753-2471. Educational guide service in a gem of a museum devoted to the ancient civilizations of the Near East.

Museum of Science & Industry, 57th St. & South Shore Dr., MU 4-1414. Senior citizens and a few college students work as part-time guides. Minimum wage to fit social security requirements. Students vie for the available jobs—apply in fall for following summer.

Field Museum of Natural History, Roosevelt Rd. & Lake Shore Dr., 922-9410. Always needs dedicated volunteers, especially retired professionals or anyone with a lifetime interest in archaeology, zoology, geology, botany. Also library work, research editing, photographing specimens, taking special visitors on tours. Volunteers recognized yearly with reception.

USO, 64 E. Randolph, 726-3082. If your only notion of USO is based on old World War II films, this center will astonish. Some 200-300 young servicemen from Great Lakes Naval Training Center, Fort Sheridan, Glenview Naval Air Base, and Chanute Air Force Base use it as headquarters for involvement in a number of volunteer projects including tutoring programs, ecology projects, and work with handicapped children, wounded patients in military hospitals, senior citizens. Most-wanted civilian volunteers: young women who can work on a flexible time schedule. USO wishes more young black women and young women from ethnic backgrounds would volunteer. The former would help attract more black servicemen, and the latter would add cross-cultural dimensions. You must be 18 and a high school graduate; expect to be interviewed.

INDEX